MW00776736

GOD'S ROAD TO
FINANCIAL
FREEDOM

Harrison
WEALTH
Shippensburg, PA

BILLY EPPERHART

GOD'S ROAD TO
FINANCIAL
FREEDOM

SIMPLE STEPS TO DESTROY DEBT,
BUILD WEALTH, AND LIVE FREE!

Published by Harrison House Publishers
Shippensburg, PA 17257

ISBN 13 TP: 978-1-6803-1878-4

ISBN 13 eBook: 978-1-6803-1879-1

For Worldwide Distribution, Printed in the U.S.A.

1 2 3 4 5 6 7 8 / 26 25 24 23 22

CONTENTS

INTRODUCTION

And you shall remember the Lord your God, for it is He who gives you power to get wealth, that He may establish His covenant which He swore to your fathers, as it is this day.

—Deuteronomy 8:18

It is time for the Body of Christ to wake up. God wants to partner with you to bring the Kingdom of Heaven into every sphere of culture. After all, Christianity was never meant to stay inside of the Church. When we integrate our faith, finances, and work, we recognize the power God has over every area of our lives. Money is a tool that can be leveraged to spread God's love in big ways, but unfortunately many Christians have not been wise when it comes to financial matters. But God has a much better plan for you!

God gives you the power to get wealth just as He did for the Israelites in Deuteronomy 8:18. Notice that the scripture doesn't say that God gives wealth; it says God provides the *power* to get it. He will give you the knowledge, the strategies, the expertise, and the help you need to be successful.

When talking about *God's Road to Financial Freedom*, it's important to unpack what financial freedom is. On the one hand, financial freedom is the literal point where passive income from investments exceeds expenses. When you are financially free, you don't have to work a job if you don't want to. Your investments pay you, and you can fully devote your time and resources to whatever God has called you to do. However, financial freedom has a second definition that is perhaps even more important. It is an attitude free from financial worries. As Christians, that freedom comes from the knowledge that God is our Provider, so we have everything we need.

Jesus spoke about this kind of freedom often. Perhaps most notably in the scriptures is found in Matthew 6:25-27:

> Therefore I tell you, do not worry about your life, what you will eat or drink; or about your body, what you will wear. Is not life more than food, and the body more than clothes? Look at the birds of the air; they do not sow or reap or store away in barns, and yet your heavenly Father feeds them. Are you not much more valuable than they? Can any one of you by worrying add a single hour to your life? (NIV)

Here's the thing—the Bible warns against the love of money a lot. However, most people only think about the danger that presents to people who are extremely wealthy, not those who are scrounging to make ends meet. On the contrary, Jesus knew that worrying about money is a major way that people become a slave to it. Finances can easily consume your thoughts and energies. During my time as a financial consultant and a pastor, I've noticed that many Christians are aware that

God wants them blessed, but they do not understand *how* to walk in that blessing. That changes now!

For several years, I tried to discover a method to explain the wealth building process in a comprehensive way. I wanted to show people the "how-to" side of prospering! Finally, after many years of experience, discussion, learning, and petitioning God, I grabbed ahold of some insights that helped me and will help you. The teaching in this book is as practical as it is spiritual. You will receive tools that will empower you to become financially free as well as the biblical foundation for why and how God calls us to steward our finances.

My heart in writing this book is to teach you how to break the hold money has over your life so you can be free to serve God. How awesome would it be to have all you need and, according to 2 Corinthians 9:8, be able to give to every good cause. That's a good place to be. *More importantly, it's where God wants you to be.*

As you learn how to manage and control your finances, you will become the master of your money.

Even more significantly, you will learn how to serve God and live more fully.

Here's the bottom line, friend. Changing your financial picture is not always easy, but it is simple. Partner with God, put the principles you are about to learn to work, and start walking *God's Road to Financial Freedom*.

—Billy Epperhart

CHAPTER 1

THE TRIPLE-X FACTOR:

A 30,000-FOOT VIEW OF WEALTH

Let's be honest—understanding your finances can be complicated. There are so many angles to approach the topic from and different perspectives to consider. You may be hesitant to believe that you can even build substantial wealth at all. My goal is not only to convince you that you can, but to show you how to do so as well. After my fair share of trial and error through the years, God revealed a financial theory to me that changed the way I looked at money. It helped me go from being mastered by my money to becoming the master of my money! I call this tool the Triple-X Factor.

To give you a brief introduction, the Triple-X Factor has three phases:

1. The First X: The point where your income becomes greater than your expenses.

2. The Second X: The point where your passive income (money from investments) becomes greater than your expenses. This phase is also called financial freedom.

3. The Third X: The point where you can give away 100 percent of your reinvested passive income and some of the assets themselves to good causes.

The purpose of the Triple-X Factor is to move people from indebted to wealthy. It does this by reversing the power of interest. When you are in debt, interest rates cause you to pay more over time. When you are an investor, you gain from the interest that's paid to you over time. Anyone can build wealth with The Triple-X Factor. However, in order to change your financial picture, you must first change your financial outlook.

A DIFFERENT PERSPECTIVE

As mentioned in the introduction, I struggled to discover a method to explain the wealth building process in a complete way for several years. Looking back, I realize that the solution came when I got a different view of the problem. What I really desired was a 30,000-foot view of wealth. Let me explain. Most of the teachings I heard about finances were too specific. They would focus on one element, such as debt elimination, and provide no context on what to do after that point. Or, they would provide great insights on investing but no direction on how to attain the money to implement their strategies. I couldn't connect all of the teachings—it was overwhelming! I felt like I was standing a few inches away from a huge elephant. Let me explain.

Imagine that someone had never seen an elephant before. They approach the animal and only see the trunk. Someone asks them, "What is an elephant?" and they say, "Oh, an elephant is a hose! Or perhaps they only saw the side of the elephant. They might say, "An elephant is a wall." Maybe they only saw the tail and said, "An elephant is a rope!"

It is easy to associate the whole of something solely with what's in our immediate perspective. If we do not reflect on how we conceptualize money, we may confine ourselves to a narrative that is incomplete. Many times, we set our own limits in our mind without realizing it. The person who saw an elephant for the first time associated the entire elephant with one part. You and I know the truth is that an elephant is more than a trunk, a side, or a tail. For a long time, I struggled to fit all of the different lessons on wealth building into a cohesive idea.

If I learned something that was associated with debt freedom, I'd relegate it to the debt-freedom compartment of my brain. If I listened to a teaching on investing, I'd stick it in the investment section. All the while, a part of me knew that building wealth was much more than eliminating debt. I knew the metaphorical trunk was attached to an elephant. Eventually, I realized something important. Debt and wealth have a common denominator—both are related to how we handle money. That one fact gave me my 30,000-foot view and enabled me to see the "whole elephant." I began to see the entirety of the problem, and the groundwork was laid for me to see the entirety of the solution. It was at that point that God gave me the Triple-X Factor.

Debt and wealth have a common denominator— both are related to how we handle money.

From that moment forward, I began to look at money differently. The Triple-X Factor enabled me to truly teach others how to master their money. Debt no longer would be a choke hold around their necks, and wealth building would no longer be just a dream. This was a turning point for me. Let this be a turning point for you as well.

~~~~~~~~~~~~~~~~~~~~~~~~~~~~

The Triple-X Factor enabled me to truly teach others how to master their money. Debt no longer would be a choke hold around their necks, and wealth building would no longer be just a dream.

~~~~~~~~~~~~~~~~~~~~~~~~~~~~

THREE KINDS OF MONEY

Money is not your problem, and it's not your enemy. If you want to master money, you must understand how to make it work for you. The Triple-X Factor focuses on three kinds of money, or three ways of collecting and putting it to work. *First-X income* is the starting point where you work a job to earn a salary. *Second-X income* is a place of great freedom where you collect and manage assets that pay you. *Third-X income* is a place of philanthropy where you give away most of your income.

THIRD X
Money that
WORKS WITHOUT YOU
Purpose
-Philanthrophy
-Kingdom Investing
-Multiple Assets
-Preserving Wealth
-Growing Wealth
-City/Nation Transformation
Type:
-Absentee Asset Income
Category:
-Investor

SECOND X
Money that
WORKS FOR YOU
Purpose:
-Tithe/Offering
-Foundational Wealth
-Asset Building
Type:
-Asset Income
Category:
-Business Owner
-Investor

FIRST X
Money that you
WORK FOR
Purpose:
-Tithe/Offering
-Asset Building
-Live Out of
Type:
-Job
Category:
-Employee
-Self Employed
-Non-leveraged income

The First X

First-X income is the payment you receive from an employer for your time and value. The majority of people's money comes from this tier, also known as "non-leveraged income" because of the direct correlation between time and a paycheck. People in the First-X category are usually employees, but they could also be self-employed.

For example, when I receive honorariums for speaking on wealth building, I receive non-leveraged income. This is because there is a direct correlation between the time I speak and the amount I get paid. However, when I sell my products after I speak, the profits count as leveraged income. This is because I spent a specific amount of time creating the products, and that specific amount of time has paid me a hundred times over. Most of the time, I make more money selling product than speaking. In this way, I have leveraged myself because people can read and hear what I teach without me being present.

The Second X

Second-X income is what we call asset income, or leveraged income. An example of asset income would be the rent collected from an investment property or dividends paid from stocks. Second-X income is sometimes called foundational wealth; it can be used to build more assets.

People at the Second-X tier are usually business owners or investors. They still work, but instead of working as an employee, they spend their time as asset managers. At the Second X, people have the option to take or leave their First-X income because their assets generate enough money to meet their needs. Some people choose to keep their jobs, while others choose to march into full-time asset management.

The Third X

Third-X income is abundant, generous, and even excessive. Needless to say, Third-X income is beyond what an individual needs to live on. At this level, an individual has multiple assets and is focused on preserving and growing wealth. At this level, people can partner with God and really make a difference with their finances—even transforming entire cities and nations. God wants to bless us on the Road to Financial Freedom so that we can bless others as well.

You can reach this Third-X tier and re-invest your excess wealth, give it away, or a form a strategy that is a combination of both. At this level, the point is that you can receive a social and spiritual return in addition to your financial returns. The graphic below illustrates how money flows throughout the Triple-X Factor.

WHERE WEALTH IS BUILT

Notice the level where wealth is built in the chart above. In the First X, a person trades their time and talents for money, and he or she is paid a fixed amount. In the Second X, the person manages assets and, in return, is paid significantly more. In other words, with First-X income, there is a one-time investment and a one-time payment. Wealth is built in the Second-X and Third-X levels because the one-time investment pays out repeatedly.

Another factor to consider with First-X income is that one-for-one ratio changes if a person enjoys an extremely high-paying career. For example, let's say a movie star is given a starring role in a one-time movie and receives $40 million. The actor would likely invest the same amount of time and labor that most people do on their jobs, but the actor gets paid significantly more. That's a desirable set up, for sure, but most people invest once and get paid once. That's why it's important to learn how to build Second-X income.

Over time, there is exponential growth as a person creates or acquires assets in the second tier. Building wealth is attainable for anyone who implements the right strategies and systems, so the sky is the limit for you! Don't wonder if you can reach this point—you can. Commit to the goal, have faith, and as you do your part, God will do His.

CHAPTER 2

WHERE YOU ARE
AND WHERE YOU ARE HEADED

Your financial future begins with understanding where you are right now. You need a firm grasp on the money you have coming in and the money you have going out. From there, you can decide how to allocate your budget. The Triple-X Factor will help you track your debt and establish a trajectory.

For example, statistics show that the average American household faces a staggering $145,000 in debt.[1] For some states it's higher and for some lower, but it's a good starting point for our illustration. At the same time, the median family income in the U.S. is

$79,900.[2] When you look these facts of indebtedness square in the face, it's very obvious that the typical household in the U.S. has a lot more money going out every month than it does coming in.

So, we are left with a major question: How can someone spend more per year than they make? The answer is debt, and unfortunately, it's pretty easy to obtain. The culprit is consumer credit. It allows us to easily buy things that immediately depreciate. We can buy items like televisions and clothes because we have credit cards or other types of installment accounts. Therefore, in America, it's exceptionally easy to spend more than you make.

DOES GOD WANT YOU TO BUILD WEALTH?

Financial issues like debt hinder Christians from walking in the full measure of their God-given freedom. Debt holds you back, but the issue runs deeper than the debt itself. Debt can be overcome, and we'll show you a real easy way to do that in subsequent chapters.

Rather, a person's mindset about wealth is often what holds them back. Many Christians do not think of building wealth, or building anything, for that matter, as being related to their faith. The reality is that God wants to be radically and intimately involved in the practical side of your life!

When God drops the occasional financial miracle onto a Christian's lap, many of them think that is the full measure of heavenly wealth. I call this a manna mindset, a phrase that comes from the Israelites' journey into the Promised Land in the Old Testament. We can learn a lot about God's will for our lives through this story. To briefly recap, God promises a man named Abraham that he is going to be a great nation, that he is going to be given a land, a place to live, and that through him all of the nations will be blessed. That promise is called the Abrahamic Covenant, and it reveals God's desire to have a relationship with humanity. However, years after the Abrahamic Covenant was made, the nation of Israel was enslaved by the Egyptians. This lasted for about 400 years. The Book of Exodus details how God miraculously rescued the Israelites out from slavery in

Egypt. Just a few days into their journey, however, the Israelites got hungry and focused on the negative:

> Then the whole congregation of the children of Israel complained against Moses and Aaron in the wilderness. And the children of Israel said to them, "Oh, that we had died by the hand of the Lord in the land of Egypt, when we sat by the pots of meat and when we ate bread to the full! For you have brought us out into this wilderness to kill this whole assembly with hunger" (Exodus 16:2-3).

God's response to their complaining wasn't angry. In His kindness, He proved how faithful, kind, and trustworthy He was by raining down bread from heaven that tasted like wafers with honey. They called it manna. This happened every day (except the Sabbath) that the Israelites were in the wilderness for the entire 40 years!

The manna was undoubtedly a miracle. However, I don't think it represented the full measure of His plans for His people. It was a stepping stone to something greater. For a God who created every food in existence, manna was the minor leagues. Can you imagine surviving off of wafer crackers for 40 years?

However, God in all His wisdom knew that manna was what the Israelites needed at the time. I don't think they were equipped in their mindset to handle a bigger blessing yet. Their journey to the Promised Land was a time when God refined their trust and obedience. He had to "get the Egypt out of them," so to speak—a little hunger made them wish they were slaves again! (Before you judge them, how often do we crave the captivity of comfort over God's will for our lives?)

So, a manna mindset is based in spiritual immaturity. Someone with a manna mindset constantly asks, "Are You there, God? If so, prove it!" It's okay to start here. We all do. However, we all reflect the image of God, our Provider, too. As we grow in spiritual maturity, He moves us out of a manna mentality so we can provide for others like He does. When you move out of a manna mentality, you become a producer, not just a consumer. In the following passage, you will see how the Israelites underwent this process.

THE PRODUCE OF THE LAND

> *While the people of Israel were encamped at Gilgal, they kept the Passover on the fourteenth day of the month in the evening on the plains of Jericho. And the day after the Passover, on that very day, they ate of the produce of the land, unleavened cakes and parched grain. And the manna ceased the day after they ate of the produce of the land. And there was no longer manna for the people of Israel, but they ate of the fruit of the land of Canaan that year* (Joshua 5:10-12 ESV).

This passage is pregnant with revelation. The Israelites' 40-year journey through the wilderness and into the Promised Land was over. They made it. Their new season was initiated by eating produce from their new home. Now they didn't eat crackers that tasted like honey—they built houses in a land that was flowing with it (see Deut. 31:20)! The meal signified two things: the fulfillment of God's promise, and the Israelites' spiritual growth.

After a time of testing in the wilderness, God had brought the Israelites to a point of spiritual maturity. Now, they were ready to build something with Him rather than solely receiving. Now that they were in the Promised Land, they didn't need manna anymore. They could cultivate their own gardens, raise their own livestock, and serve at their own tables. Getting the Israelites to the Promised Land wasn't the end of the story—it was just the beginning.

YOUR PROMISED LAND

Similarly, God has called you into a Promised Land. There is a divine plan and promise for your life, and just like the Israelites, there will be a time of testing and wandering as well. While you seek out God's calling for your life, wait, and develop your character, there will be seasons when you are more dependent on God's daily provision than others. However, God's will for your life is for you to graduate beyond manna—that you would learn to obey and trust Him in the wilderness so that you can prosper in the land that He has for you.

Getting to the Promised Land is essential for receiving the promise. However, we can't continue to wander and feel entitled to manna as our birthright. The manna isn't the birthright, it's an appetizer. The land is the inheritance—the main course. When Jesus said, "the kingdom of heaven is at hand" (Matt. 4:17), it meant that part of our inheritance is activated now. Being saved and redeemed in Christ means that we get to share in the vision God has for the world and partner as His stewards and representatives.

We are called to create environments that serve as an invitation for others to taste and see that the Lord is good. We are commissioned to do as God did. Not only to reap from the harvest of our work, but to plant and feed God's sheep—the people God loves, whether they know Him yet or not. That is why it is important for Christians to learn how to build wealth.

Financial freedom equips Christians with the resources and time to fully dive into their Promised Land.

It's nice to receive financial miracles. They build our faith and give us confidence that God is a good Provider who is invested in our lives. However, at some point wouldn't you like to be the one God uses to bestow financial miracles? Financial freedom is one of the ways that Christians can move beyond manna and cultivate a land that provides blessings for others.

VISUALS HELP

Take a look at the next chart to get a picture of where you are and where you are headed financially. Remove the guesswork and plug in the real numbers that apply to your finances.

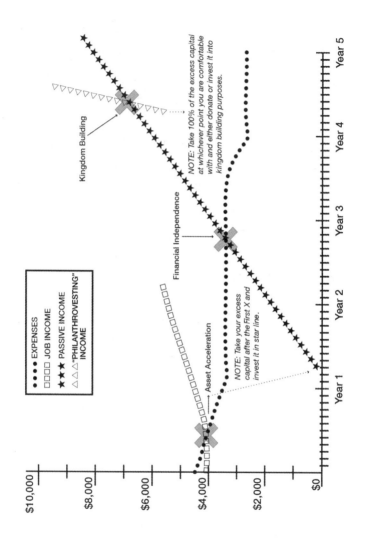

GOD'S ROAD TO FINANCIAL FREEDOM

Scan the QR code to download and fill out your own chart.

Year 1   Year 2   Year 3   Year 4   Year 5

$0

Each dot represents one month of expenses. So for this illustration, at the beginning, we have about $4,500 going out each month.

BUILDING YOUR PERSONAL CHART

It's important to position yourself to build wealth, and an important move in that direction is to develop your own personal chart following the steps below.

1. Plot your expenses each month.

To fill out your own chart, you need to be very honest about your expenses. Start with the month you're in right now. Begin to chart your monthly expenses. For instance, let's say you start in April, and the total outgo of expenses in March was $2,500. You would place an asterisk at the $2,500 mark. At the end of the month, you'd place another asterisk to represent how much you spent in April.

Once you start implementing the tools in this book, you should see your expenses go down. This will allow you to start paying off your debt while learning how to handle your finances more effectively. However, life happens. Expenses don't always come down. Sometimes it is a result of your spending habits, and sometimes it's just a result of life's accidents or the market. Be patient with yourself and continue to keep track of how much you're spending. This cultivates awareness, and awareness typically catalyzes change.

2. Plot your income each month.

Chart your first month's income in the same way that you charted your first monthly expenses. This line will probably stay horizontal for a while. Over time, though, the goal is that you'll grow in your career, adopt some side hustles, or launch into entrepreneurship. These factors obviously cause your income to rise!

3. Build your First X.

Some people are at the First X right off the bat, which means that they have more income than expenses. If this is the case, they can start building the Second X. However, for most people, the First X is in rougher shape. They have more expenses than they do income. In order to build the First X, monthly expenses need to come down.

Most people will be able to start controlling their expenses, especially their consumer debt, before they start to increase their income. That's completely normal. Start working on your expenses immediately by cutting things out, making extra cash, or driving down debt.

When it comes to your income, remember this: you take value to the marketplace—not time. Getting paid per hour makes it easy to fall into a mindset that minimizes your work to a time exchange. I like to believe that money is attracted, not pursued. So, when you start to work on yourself harder than you do on your job, you will get paid more for your job because you have become more valuable. As expenses go down and income rises, you begin to form the First X. Now, you are in a position to start building wealth.

4. Gain assets.

Prevent backsliding by graphing your income and expense lines every month so you can monitor exactly where you are. This information keeps you accountable and knowledgeable. Making critical decisions about your finances without data is like flying a plane with your eyes closed. You must have a data dashboard to arrive at the correct destination.

Making critical decisions about your finances without data is like flying a plane with your eyes closed.

For example, as the First X forms, you'll notice that a gap develops between the black income line and red expense line. That gap represents excess capital that you now have available. Your decision about what you do with that capital determines your trajectory for wealth building. If you choose to spend it, you aren't getting into any more debt, but you're not building any wealth either. Which is more important—what you want now, or what you want most? The real key to building wealth is to invest the extra into income producing assets. For some people it may take several years to reach a point where they have excess capital to deploy or invest. That's okay! Stick with it, and you will get there. In the beginning you probably won't have enough to make a larger investment such as a piece of real estate, but you can open a Roth IRA or other investment account (more on that later).

A while back, I was teaching on real estate at a conference at the Omni Hotel in Dallas, Texas. When I finished, two huge guys, about 6 feet 5 inches, came up to me. They said, "We're ready to invest in real estate!"

Which is more important: what you want now, or what you want most?

They were pumped from the talk, so I looked at them and said, "Well, do you have any money?"

"Well, no, we don't have any money. But we are excited and ready to invest!"

I suppressed a laugh and seriously offered, "When you have $10,000 through whatever means in your possession, call me. I'll fly to Dallas at my expense and teach you how to buy your first investment property."

Six months later, one of the guys called me. He had $10,000, so I flew out to Texas to fill out my end of the bargain. Today he owns more than 60 individual properties—multi-family units and single-family houses.

If you don't have money to invest, don't worry. Put yourself in a position to invest by saving your excess capital. A simple illustration of an asset that brings income is a rental property with positive cash flow. You rent your property out and receive income from their rent—enough to pay off your mortgage and pocket some extra. The more of these types of investments you accumulate, the more the snowball will start rolling in the right direction.

Note: you can start to build assets even before your reach the First X. If you're not in a financial position to acquire assets, you can create them. An example of creating an asset is starting an eBay or Etsy shop, tutoring, freelancing, or fashioning any kind of business outside of your day job that provides immediate cash flow. Then, you can use that cash flow to start investing or to pay off debt.

5. Build the Second X.

Again, the key to the Triple X is to put your excess capital into things that produce income for you. Your knowledge about how to invest well and returns will continue to grow. Here's what happens once this occurs:

The dotted expense line continues to go down, and the starred asset line continues to grow. When they cross over, it means that your cost of living is covered by passive income! You can now quit your job if you'd like. By God's grace and help, I was able to reach financial independence in two and a half years. But for some people, it may take a lot longer than that. Remember—everyone's pace in the race of life is different.

A lot of people ask me what their first big goal should be when they start to build wealth, and I always tell them what the Triple-X Factor says: Your first *big* goal should be to replace your active/earned income with passive income. That's the key to start experiencing financial independence. So, why do most people never reach that point?

For the longest time, the financial industry in America has told people to put their extra money in a 401K, an IRA, or some type of retirement account. Businesses back this practice by matching some percentage of what their employees put into a retirement account. It is wise to save for retirement—hear me on that—but to put all your eggs in that basket sets you up for a slow wealth building process.

~~~~~~~~~~~~~~~~~~~~~

Many people who retire with a decent portfolio have never taken the time to learn how badly taxes could bite them and steal their wealth.

~~~~~~~~~~~~~~~~~~~~~

Many people who retire with a decent portfolio have never taken the time to learn how badly taxes could bite them and steal their wealth. When they retire, they end up paying more taxes in what we call "tax-deferred accounts" than they were paying when they were actually working and making a salary. The minute they start pulling that money out of those normal IRAs and 401Ks, they have to pay earned-income tax on that money. After all is said and done, they end up having much less than they thought. (There are a few ways to form a retirement account that gets around those taxes. Again, more on that later.)

6. Build the Third X.

You will recall on the First X when the dotted line crossed the line of squares, a gap resulted. The same thing will happen with the Second X. Another gap will form, and it represents excess capital again. It's at that point I marked on my chart: *Quit job!*

You may ask, "When I reach that point, what will I do with new excess capital?" That is the moment you can really partner with God to build wealth. God is all about prosperity with a purpose, and this is where the Third X comes in. We talk more about this in Chapter 7.

Somewhere in your excess capital gap, you will reach a point where you can start giving all your income away and investing some of your assets for a social and spiritual impact. At this point, you are able to give far more than your 10 percent tithe. All of the income earned after the Second X can be given away.

GOD'S ROAD TO FINANCIAL FREEDOM

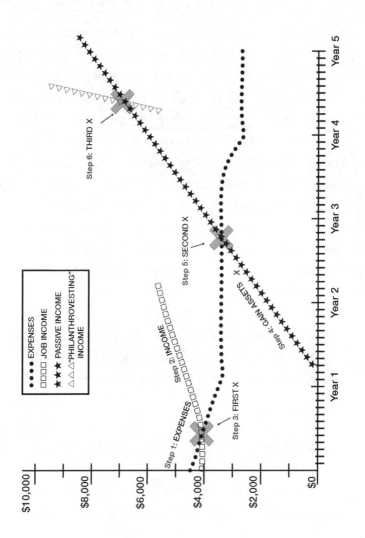

Now, you can continue to reinvest your excess capital. With this additional wealth, you can sow back into the Kingdom of God. You may think, *How would that actually work? What does that actually mean?* To recap, Third-X income is completely excess. It can all be given away to the Church, nonprofits, or you can even start an organization that gives back to the community. That's why my wife and I started WealthBuilders, our nonprofit that educates people about how to make sense of making money for making a difference. It's why we created Tricord Global, an organization that provides microfinance loans to the poor in developing nations so they can be empowered to start businesses and move out of poverty in a sustainable way. Now that we've built wealth, we use it to restore goodness and justice to the earth, thus fulfilling Matthew 6:10: "Thy Kingdom come, thy will be done in earth, as it is in heaven" (KJV).

SUMMARY

Over the years, I've developed a financial theory that helps people go from being mastered by money to mastering their money. Deuteronomy 8:18 states that God gives us the power to get wealth, and I believe He revealed the Triple-X Factor as a tool to do so.

First-X income is the point where you put in time and value, and you get paid for that time and value. Most people are at this First X. Second-X income is what we call asset income. People at this tier are usually business owners or investors. Third-X income goes beyond both of these. The amount at this income level is abundant and excessive—beyond what you need. The purpose of Third-X income is to be given away—God doesn't give prosperity without a purpose.

NOTES

1. Bill Fay, "Demographics of Debt," Debt.org, October 19, 2021, https://www.debt.org/faqs/americans-in-debt/demographics.

2. U.S. Department of Housing and Urban Development, "Estimated Median Family Incomes for Fiscal Year (FY) 2021," Huduser.gov, April 1, 2021, https://www.huduser.gov/portal/datasets/il/il21/Medians2021.pdf.

CHAPTER 3

SEVEN STEPS
TO FINANCIAL FREEDOM

Now that you've gotten an overview of the wealth building process, it's time to take a closer look at each step. Eliminating debt and building wealth is all about being intentional with your money. In other words, you must take purposeful actions and be committed to those actions. No financial ruts allowed! Anyone is only ever seven steps away from financial freedom. With that, here are the seven steps!

STEP 1: ESCALATE

The first step to financial freedom is to *escalate* your ability to earn. I had the opportunity to share this advice with several government ministers in Kampala, Uganda, when they attended one of my Triple-X Factor presentations. I was fascinated by the questions asked during this gathering of roughly two dozen leaders. One young man asked a simple yet poignant question: "What do we do here in Kampala when we don't have the resources or capital to start businesses?"

No financial ruts allowed! Anyone is only ever seven steps away from financial freedom.

In Uganda, it is much harder to access capital. And even if you can, the interest rates are astronomical. However, there was something that the young man could do. I explained to him that the first step was to increase his knowledge about business and how to make money. I told him to seek education in any form. I advise you to do the same. There are many people in many areas of enterprise, me included, who give out free content on how to do business and build wealth. Take advantage of the wealth of knowledge and expertise that is available in today's day and age. Read blogs, books, and magazines. Listen to podcasts. Watch videos. Find mentors, attend networking events, and register for conferences.

As I mentioned earlier, you get paid for value—not for time. So, as you increase your knowledge, understanding, and wisdom regarding business and financial matters, you increase your ability to earn because your value increases. You will have more skills to offer as an employee, or more business acumen to bring to your own company. In other words: The more you learn, the more you earn.

STEP 2: ELIMINATE

The second step to financial freedom is to *eliminate* your consumer debt. Consumer debt is an impasse in our ability to increase our wealth. When you have debt, you pay interest, and that interest takes away from the money that you could be used to build wealth. In other words, you're actually building someone else's wealth when you pay interest. That's why it's very important to eliminate consumer debt.

As you escalate your ability to earn, your income will go up and you'll be able to allocate more toward debt payments. Consequentially your expenses will go down because you will be eliminating consumer debt. These two steps—escalating your ability to earn and eliminating consumer debt—are how you reach the First X.

You might ask, "Will these two steps cause me to build wealth?" No, of course not! You won't build wealth simply by eliminating consumer debt, but these two steps will put you in a position to start building wealth.

The amount of consumer debt in America is off the charts. The total outstanding U.S. revolving debt (including credit card debt but not mortgage debt) in 2021 was $996 billion (2013 was $847 billion).[1] Our debt is equal to the gross domestic product of Belgium and Denmark—combined. Yet, in the United States, we wonder why we cannot get ahead. (In the next chapter, I'll walk you through how to eliminate consumer debt in nine steps.)

STEP 3: ACCUMULATE

Having initiated the first two steps, it's time to move forward to the third step toward financial freedom, which is to *accumulate.* Accumulating wealth is the beginning of the Second X. At this step, you should establish an emergency fund and begin saving for a home. More specifically, I advise you to create a savings account and stock it up for several months. If you can, use ten percent of your income for an emergency fund. When you have three to six months of living expenses saved in this account, start saving for a home if you don't already have one.

Of course, not everyone will decide to create an emergency fund, but I strongly encourage you to have a source of cash besides your credit cards to use just in case the need arises. You need to save for emergencies because emergencies arise unexpectedly. If you are prepared, they might only feel like a small bump in the road. If you are not prepared, they can wipe out money needed for other expenses and create long-standing financial problems. Setting money aside for a rainy day is just good common sense.

Once you have an amount in your emergency fund that you're comfortable with, you use 10 percent of your income to save up for a home instead. If you plan to live in an area for a while, have the financial means, and can get a fair deal for a property, buying a home is a much better option than renting. When you buy a house, you own an asset that appreciates in value. When you rent, you never see that money again.

As of 2021, The Federal Housing Administration (FHA) allows first-time homebuyers to purchase a

Libability

home for as little as 3.5 percent down. There are also programs for first-time home buyers that provide down payment assistance, which can come in the form of a grant or a loan. Saving for a home is a great way to position yourself to build wealth!

STEP 4: PARTICIPATE

After you have successfully saved for a home, it's time to take the fourth step and *participate*. In other words, you need to start building an asset base. Two of the easiest ways to get started are to open a Roth IRA and buy your own home.

Homeownership really is the cornerstone of the American dream. For centuries, it has symbolized building a life, security, and place for oneself in the world. In any country, owning a personal home is a significant milestone. However, homeownership has much more to offer than warm and fuzzy feelings. A home doesn't just provide physical shelter—it provides financial shelter as well.

Liability

When you pay a mortgage, your money goes toward an asset that you own. If you give it enough time, your home's value will appreciate as well. This simply means that it will be worth far more than you paid for it one day. And, when you're ready to move on to a new space, you can rent out your old home and create a passive income stream while still retaining your asset. It's just a smart move! There are several other advantages to purchasing your own home. One is that you will have a capital gains exemption. This means that if the home is your primary residence, you can make up to a $500,000 profit on your house, tax-free. Not tax deferred, but free! This is a wonderful thing.

The second low-risk way to build an asset base is to invest in a Roth IRA. This type of IRA is almost always the best way to go if you are under a certain income threshold. The threshold typically changes each year, but in 2021 it was under $125,000 for individuals and under $198,000 for married people filing jointly.[2] So, I especially encourage younger people to open one. Here's why—all of the earnings in a Roth IRA (typically a 7 to 10 percent return each year) are tax free. Plus, you can borrow the money you put in (not including the earnings) with no penalty or issue. For instance, you might use the funds for a down payment on a house.

After I went through the process of participation and bought a home, my financial picture really accelerated. After that, it wasn't too terribly long until I completed the most real estate transactions I've ever done in a single year—about 200! But remember, before I could *accelerate*, I had to *participate*. Before you can build significant wealth, you have to understand how to take the first steps. If your plan is to build wealth through real estate investing like I did, you must buy a home first. I bought an investment property through borrowing against the equity I built in my personal home. After I sustained significant growth in my investment properties, I actually closed my IRA (despite a substantial financial penalty) and used that cash to invest in my real estate business.

If you get these two things started—purchasing a home and opening a Roth IRA—you will have built a solid asset base to help you get to the Second X.

STEP 5: ACCELERATE

The fifth step to financial freedom is to *accelerate,* and there are three primary ways to accomplish this: invest in real estate, invest in the stock market, and invest in your own business. Look with me at these concepts below in more detail.

Invest in Real Estate

It's important to learn how to invest in real estate in addition to the purchase of your personal home. In fact, 90 percent of the world's millionaires have been created by investing in real estate.[3] This doesn't necessarily mean that these individuals receive passive income from their real estate, but it does mean that they hold their wealth in the value of their properties.

For example, you might hear about millionaire or billionaire celebrities like Oprah Winfrey who own 10 mansions around the world and wonder about their rationale behind owning multiple estates. Most of the time, it doesn't come from a desire to jet-set around the world and show off their wealth. Typically, the primary motivation for owning multiple homes is for tax planning purposes.

~~~~~~~~~~~~~~~~~~~~~~

It's important to learn how to invest in real estate in addition to the purchase of your personal home.

~~~~~~~~~~~~~~~~~~~~~~

This concept is pretty common among the wealthy. They set up a real estate business because they receive so much income from their business that the taxes would be astronomical. So, they roll that cash over into real estate. Then, they write off the depreciation of their properties to shelter the income they make. This is brilliant wealth building via tax planning! Another bonus is that real estate typically retains its value better than other investments.

Invest in the Stock Market

Another option to build wealth is to invest in the stock market, although it's my least favorite of the three ways to accelerate your wealth. The most important thing to learn about investing in the stock market is how to position yourself so you don't lose money.

Warren Buffett, the sage of Omaha and an American business magnate, investor, and philanthropist, said the secret to making money is not losing money. Personally, I have lost a lot of money in the stock market, but the good news is that I had the money to lose. The better news is that, overall, I still made more than I lost. When I started out, I lost a lot of money because I wasn't patient in step one of the seven steps to financial freedom—escalate. In other words, I didn't take the time to build my knowledge, understanding, and wisdom in the right areas.

Own Your Own Business

The third way to accelerate your wealth is to invest in your own business. Business is different from investing in real estate and the stock market because when you properly build a business, that business actually replaces your First-X income. When you invest in the real estate and the stock market, you simply invest the excess capital from your First-X (earned) income. Some people are able to do both. For instance, consider Peyton Manning. The football quarterback retired in 2016 after 14 seasons with the Indianapolis Colts and four with the Denver Broncos. During the time he actively played for a team, he earned his First-X income, although that figure was a whole lot more than most of us will ever make in the First-X tier. In addition to his sizable contract, he also earned a lot of money doing commercials for Papa John's and Best Buy. (He also purchased a couple of Papa John's franchises.) These things have nothing to do with actually playing football, but they have a lot to do with his financial picture. In other words, he set up a business to receive income from advertising.

You can go straight from the First X to the Second X and build a business this way, but it's hard because you need to have some sort of consistent income in your life. Most of the time, it takes even the most successful businesses about three years to become profitable. So, most people need to use the First-X income from their job to invest in their business before their business is able to generate passive income and be their sole source of revenue.

To summarize, you can accelerate your income by investing in real estate, the stock market, and businesses. Here are five forms of passive income that can help you accelerate:

- Rent from real estate
- Capital distributions from a business
- Dividends from stocks
- Interest from bonds and CDs
- Royalties from songs, books, etc.

STEP 6: EMANCIPATE

After you accelerate your passive income generation, it's only a matter of time until you emancipate! In other words, you will become financially free because your passive income will have replaced your earned income. So at this point, you can leave your job if you desire and live off your assets instead.

Now that I'm emancipated, so to speak, I don't need to work a job. However, I love teaching, and I love traveling to different parts of the world to teach. I also feel like God has called me to be the CEO of Andrew Wommack Ministries and Charis Bible College. The difference is that I don't have to do these things for the money. I can do them whether they're profitable or not because the passive income from my assets will take care of my needs, my family's needs, and more.

STEP 7: DONATE

The seventh step to financial freedom is to *donate*. This step represents the Third X, the phase where we are able to give 100 percent of our excess income to other people. This includes donations, but it can also include biblically responsible or social impact investments. Social impact investing is a form of investing where you receive an annual return for investing in causes that also produce a positive social and/or environmental return. In this phase, you don't invest for the money; you invest because it offers aid and empowerment to the people you're helping. Once you receive your financial return, you can reinvest it into similar causes. It's an endless cycle of good!

The goal of the Third X is to use the money you've made to repeatedly make a difference. It's the vision at our nonprofit, WealthBuilders, and it's my hope for you, too. You financially position yourself not just to enjoy wealth but to impact the Kingdom of God!

> **You financially position yourself not just to enjoy wealth but to impact the Kingdom of God!**

SUMMARY

There are seven steps to financial freedom: escalate, eliminate, accumulate, participate, accelerate, emancipate, and donate.

- *Escalate* by increasing your ability to earn.
- *Eliminate* consumer debt.
- *Accumulate* and move forward by saving for emergencies and saving for a home.

- Now that you've saved for a home, *participate* by purchasing a home and opening a Roth IRA.
- There are three primary ways to *accelerate*: invest in real estate, invest in the stock market, and invest in your own business.
- Once the asterisks start rolling and the Second X starts forming, you can *emancipate*. This is the point of financial freedom where you can live entirely off your assets and quit your job if you'd like.
- *Donate* and invest 100 percent of your excess money into Kingdom advancement and social causes.

NOTES

1. Alexandria White, "Revolving credit debt drops to $996 billion—the lowest since the great recession," CNBC.com, September 20, 2021, https://www.cnbc.com/select/revolving-credit-debt-lowest-since-the-great-recession.

2. "2020-2021 Roth IRA Contribution Limits," Schwab.com, https://www.schwab.com/ira/roth-ira/contribution-limits.

3. Jonathan Yates, "90% of the World's Millionaires Do This to Create Wealth," thecollegeinvestor.com, October 24, 2021, https://thecollegeinvestor.com/11300/90-percent-worlds-millionaires-do-this.

CHAPTER 4

THE FIRST X:

MASTERING EARNED INCOME

For most people in the United States, there are two classifications of income according to the Internal Revenue Service (IRS). In other countries, this government authority is typically known as the Revenue of Authority, but still, the two classifications of income are the same: earned income and passive income.

Tax authorities classify First-X income as earned income. If you work a job and get paid for your time and value, you are taxed according to earned income wages, and a W-2 or a 1099 is issued for this type of income.

Second-X income is passive income, which tax authorities classify as income received from assets. For instance, these could be things like capital gains from a business, dividends from stocks, or rent from real estate property. If there's any positive cash flow from an asset, it is considered passive income, not earned income.

Consider how this works when you own a business. The salary you receive from the business is classified as earned income. But at the end of the year, you can take a capital distribution from that business, which then counts as passive income. For now, let's figure out how to master your earned income.

First-X (earned) income is represented by the line of squares in the Triple-X Factor, while the expenses are represented by the dotted line. The First X is where those two intersect. Most people in the U.S. live around the First X. In other words, they live off their job.

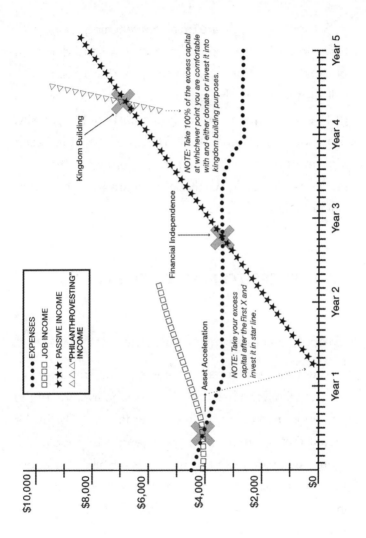

The figure shows a line graph with the vertical axis labeled in dollar amounts from $0 to $10,000 (marked at $2,000, $4,000, $6,000, $8,000, $10,000) and the horizontal axis showing Year 1 through Year 5.

Legend:
- ●●●● EXPENSES
- □□□□ JOB INCOME
- ★★★ PASSIVE INCOME
- △△△ "PHILANTHROVESTING" INCOME

Labels on the graph:
- Asset Acceleration
- Financial Independence
- Kingdom Building

NOTE: Take your excess capital after the First X and invest it in star line.

NOTE: Take 100% of the excess capital at whichever point you are comfortable with and either donate or invest it into kingdom building purposes.

So how exactly do we go about reaching the First X? How do we increase our First-X income and decrease our expenses? For most people, reaching the First X will be their starting goal in the Triple-X Factor. This goal is not to get a raise or find a better job. Typically, those perks come naturally. The true goal is to reach a point of financial preparedness from which you can really start to build wealth. Below are four steps that will help you!

FOUR STEPS TO MASTER THE FIRST X

Step 1: Become more valuable.

American entrepreneur, author, and motivational speaker Jim Rohn has said, "You are the average of the five people you spend the most time with." By this he meant that the more time you spend with people, the more like them you become. After a while, you adopt their mannerisms, sayings, and ideas until you become—in some sense—an average of these five people.

You can be pulled up or down by your associations. Of course, this does not mean you should fire all your friends, but it may be time to branch out and make some new ones. For example, in America, there are some families in their sixth generation of welfare because it's the only lifestyle they have ever known. Their environment pulls them down instead of up.

Let me ask an important question. What people have you surrounded yourself with? What are those associations doing to you? Do you influence each other for good? Do you better each other? Are you like iron sharpening iron?

> *As iron sharpens iron, so one person sharpens another* (Proverbs 27:17 NIV).

Most people's wages fall within 20 percent of their friends' wages. So, if you want to master your money, find some friends who have mastered theirs. You need to be around people who can help pull you up. If you want to earn more or gain a higher net worth, befriend people who have already attained this goal. Then, you will learn from them because friends influence each other.

Most people's wages fall within 20 percent of their friends' wages. So, if you want to master your money, find some friends who have mastered theirs.

All this boils down to one important fact that has nothing to do with money but everything to do with you. In order to enjoy an above-average income, you must become an above-average person. That's why it's important to invest in yourself more than you do in your job. As I mentioned earlier, we get paid for our value—not our time. Your company pays your salary because you hold a valuable position in the company, not because you show up from 8 a.m. to 5 p.m. Your time might be a part of that value, but it's not the whole part. Think about this. If you showed up from 8 a.m. to 5 p.m. and did nothing, would you keep that job?

Focus on increasing your value so you can increase your income. You will become more valuable by investing in yourself, so learn how to pour into yourself. Be, as Jesus said in Matthew 10:16, "Wise as serpents and innocent as doves" (ESV). Immeasurable value comes from learning how to walk in the wisdom that comes from the Word of God!

How to Invest in Yourself

Before you invest in anything monetarily, you should invest in yourself. When you invest in yourself, it means two things. The first: you are stewarding your current season to its maximum potential. The second: you are preparing in faith for what God has in your future. So, with that, here are three ways that you can invest in yourself: learn, look, and listen.

Learn

Try to read something positive and inspirational every day. A good place to start is the Bible. Connection with God is the source of all value. As the Holy Spirit speaks into your life, you will become more valuable to other people. In addition, I recommend consuming educational content twice a week. I used to advise people to read two books a week, but now there are so many informative podcasts, audiobooks, and blogs out there that the possibilities are endless. The point is, if you do this, ten years from now you will have read 1,000 books, listened to 1,000 programs, or done a mixture of the two.

Listen

God uses the successful lives of other people to show us how to walk in excellence. When we see people who are successful, we can become successful by matching their beliefs and behavior. Find wise people you can trust. Listen to them, even if their opinion runs counter to your own personal beliefs. If they are successful and you are not, hindering beliefs could be holding you back. A successful person's advice will help you grow and change, so follow it even if it's uncomfortable and unfamiliar.

You may need help finding the right people, so ask God where to look. When televangelist Robert Schuller was getting ready to build the Crystal Cathedral, his construction estimate began at nine million dollars (although the final cost of the project was doubled to $18 million before it opened its doors in 1980).[1] He went to one of his benefactors and asked him how to raise the money. The man replied, "How do you hunt a moose?"

Schuller, puzzled, replied, "I don't know how to hunt a moose."

The man told him to go and figure it out, and then he would have his solution. So, when he got home Schuller started thinking about it. He reasoned, "First of all, I must go where the moose lives. Second, I must learn the habits of a moose. Third, I'll have to learn what interests a moose. And fourth, I'd better be prepared when I hunt the moose." He took those four guidelines and used them to raise millions of dollars for the Crystal Cathedral.

You need to ask yourself how to hunt your metaphorical moose. Do your best to understand what people need and want, not just what you have to offer. If you are going to find someone who has been successful, go to a place that person frequents (not in a creepy way, of course). Then, learn the habits of that person, deduce what interests them, and come prepared whenever you encounter them.

I once had the opportunity to meet with one of the greatest success authorities in the world for five uninterrupted hours. He came to speak at my church and the next day spoke to 20,000 people in a large arena. People asked me how I was so fortunate to meet with him. The answer is simple. I learned how to hunt a moose! I wrote him the kind of letter he would respond to, so not only did he come to my church, but he would not accept any money for speaking to the congregation.

When I met with him privately, I was prepared with a 10-page list of well-thought-out questions. I journaled all his answers, and today those answers serve as an invaluable resource to me. In some areas, I learned more from him in five hours than I had learned in my previous 20 years. It's valuable and pivotal to get around people who are doing something right. Rub shoulders with them, so to speak. Learn what they are doing and why they are doing it, and it will propel you toward success.

A Recipe for Success

When my friend was battling cancer, we found a book titled *Healed of Cancer* by Dodie Osteen. Diagnosed with liver cancer, Dodie was told she had only three weeks to live. In her book, she shares the solution to getting healed. She teaches on how to model her behavior and receive healing from God. My friend did what she did, and he got the same results!

In other instances, people achieve a level of success, but they have no clue how they got there. They don't have any idea what recipe for success they used. In fact, they remind me of my wife's grandmother who could not remember the recipe for her prized tea cakes. We eat them every Christmas, so one year Becky decided that she'd better acquire the family recipe so that the tradition could live on.

"How do you make those tea cakes?" Becky asked.

"I don't know," Grandma said. "Why don't you come over and let me show you how to make those tea cakes?"

Becky watched and learned. She asked, "Grandma, how much sugar do you put in?"

"I don't know, honey," Grandma said. "I just reach in there with my hand and take this much out."

Becky watched as Grandma took some sugar from the bowl. Then, Becky put the sugar in a measuring cup to find and record the exact amount.

Grandma really did not know the recipe, but she knew all about tea cakes. At almost 90 years old, Grandma had been making tea cakes for 80 years. Becky had to work to get that recipe, but now our family will enjoy Grandma's tea cakes for generations to come.

Likewise, some people still don't know Dodie's recipe for her healing, even after reading her book. They still don't grasp what she actually did. Maybe they read that Dodie meditated on the promises in the Bible, but they didn't try it out themselves. After all, Dodie didn't mean to meditate for 10 minutes and then put down the Bible. She was encouraging people to meditate in God's Word *all day long!* When she talked about praying in the Spirit, she wasn't talking about praying for a few minutes. Dodie was talking about praying *all day long!*

You may say, "All day? But I have a family. I have work. I have things to do."

Dodie did not care what other work needed to be done. She did not care what anyone else thought. Medical science had given her a death sentence, so she focused solely on God's Word that promises life. Dodie paid close attention to the words of Proverbs 4.

> *Listen, son of mine, to what I say. Listen carefully. Keep these thoughts ever in mind; let them penetrate deep within your heart, for they will mean real life for you and radiant health* (Proverbs 4:20-22 TLB).

Dodie locked herself in her bedroom and stayed there all day to pray and meditate. Few people know what that is like. She stuck with the Word until it penetrated deep in her heart and brought forth radiant health.

If I had the opportunity to interview Dodie Osteen, I would ask questions to discover her recipe. I would ask what her path was to victory and healing. I would ask, "When the doctor said, 'You only have three weeks to live,' what was your thought process? What pictures did you see in your mind at that moment? Then, what mental pictures did you see after you spent time in the Bible? What were you feeling? What were you hearing? What new information came to you?"

Another thing I would ask Dodie is what beliefs she possessed at the time she heard her diagnosis. What did she believe about the process of meditating on and speaking the Word of God? Sometimes people speak affirmations of faith while imagining the complete opposite. So, I believe the most important thing is that Dodie believed in the process of faith, which many people miss. If we operate in faith, our faith will work every time.

When my son was a baseball pitcher at a NCAA Division 1 university, this is how I encouraged him: "When you get around guys who are successful and making it to the pros, don't ask them how they throw a curve ball," I said. "Granted, that will help you, but there are other questions you can ask that will help you a lot more. Ask them what is going on in their minds when they are on the pitcher's mound. Ask them what they are feeling, thinking, and seeing. Get their recipes!"

Some of you desire to see changes in your life that go way beyond your financial picture. Some of you want to see your teenager come back home or your marriage restored. Again, let me ask you, what images are you seeing? What are you picturing in your mind? What are you hearing and feeling? What are you believing? No matter the category, I am giving you a strategy to discover the recipe to success—to God's best for your life.

The Bible says, "Faith comes by hearing, and hearing by the Word of God" (Rom. 10:17), but you need to know what people did with the Word of God to make it work for them. Many people get depressed and ask, "Why is this happening to me?" Instead, they should be asking, "What can I do about it? What does God want me to do about it? What can God help me learn in the process of overcoming this situation? How can I beat this problem? How can I beat lack and find God's best?"

Find someone who will coach, teach, train, and mentor you, and listen to them.

Here's the point. If you want to be wealthy, take a rich person to dinner or coffee and ask them these questions: What do you believe about wealth? What kinds of things were you believing and thinking when you got started? What images were you seeing? What were you feeling? Find someone who will coach, teach, train, and mentor you, and listen to them. If you see a person you admire, invite them out so you can hear about their life and how they reached success.

Look

Success always leaves clues! One of the greatest mistakes I made as a young man was assuming how and why people became successful without ever really studying the successful people in my life. By looking and allowing God to teach us, we can learn to model the examples of those who are successful. The apostle Paul gave good advice along this line when he said, "Imitate me, just as I also imitate Christ" (1 Cor. 11:1). As we carefully look and observe, we will start to see how people function and operate, *and then* we can follow them to success.

One of the first qualified mentors I benefited from in real estate gave me a secret on how to find out if someone will be a good tenant. It's still benefiting me after all these years. He told me that one of the best ways to qualify tenants is to, if possible, see where they live before they rent from you.

Success always leaves clues!

"How can I do that?" I remember asking him.

He told me to take the lease to their house without telling them I was coming. He said when they let you inside, you will get to see how they keep house. My mentor had owned rental property for 40 years, so he knew something about tenants. I learned to humble myself, observe carefully, and imitate him. I'm so glad I did. There's someone with expertise for you to follow as well, and God will show you who it is.

Step 2: Learn to live on 80 percent.

The second step is to create (and stick to) a budget. In order to do this, you need to get really honest about your income and expenses. Make a list of what you spend money on each month (refer to old bank statements if you need them). Include rent, utilities, gas, food, subscriptions, and miscellaneous purchases. Total that number and subtract it from your monthly income. That will give you an idea of how much extra you're working with.

Then, learn how to apply the 80/20 rule. The 80/20 rule means that you use 80 percent of your income each month to pay for expenses and 20 percent to tithe and invest. I would encourage you to make it 70/30 if you're able. Here's the real breakdown:

10 percent: Tithe

There's a reason this one's first. When we surrender the first fruits of our income to God, we set ourselves up for peace and success. It helps us get it into our heads that God is our provider. Not only is God worthy of the money—he's the reason we have anything in the first place. Tithing, whether you give it to the church or donate it elsewhere, brings connection within the Body of Christ.

80 percent (or 70 percent): Use for Necessary Expenses

This includes rent, bills, loan and credit payments, food, gas, and whatever you must spend money on to survive. The beauty of this is that you can buy anything you want to, including junk if it falls into this percentage! That may not seem like a big deal, but it means that you're not going into debt.

5 percent (or 10 percent): Professionally Invest

You can professionally invest by putting a portion of your income into stocks, mutual funds, or a Roth IRA. Any investment bank can help you do this for little or no cost—you don't have to be an expert! If you're going the IRA route, make sure that you do a Roth IRA instead of a traditional IRA. With a Roth, you invest using after-tax dollars, which means you don't pay a cent in additional taxes when you take the money out. (If you're going to need the money somewhat soon, this isn't the route for you. In order to avoid fees, you need to have owned the account for at least five years and be at least 59 1/2 years of age before you make a withdrawal.)

Another important thing to remember about opening a Roth IRA is to do so at an investment bank— not a federal or state-chartered bank. A brokerage account at an investment bank will offer you a much higher level and a wider range of securities that produce a larger return.

5 percent (or 10 percent): Personally Invest

It's important to personally invest some of your money so that you know how the process works. Then, one day you'll be able to do more on your own and teach others as well. I started teaching my grandson how to personally invest when he was eight years old. I pulled him aside and said, "Brayden, Poppa is going to teach you how to invest." We went out on a

Saturday morning and found a garage sale that had an old, broken-down, red wagon. It was rusted over and missing a wheel, so we only paid $2.

We took the wagon home, and I found some black and red paint in my garage. We bought a new wheel. I let Brayden do a lot of the sanding and painting. When it looked new again, we put a "for sale" sign out in the driveway. We sold it for $20! Brayden marveled at how we turned $2 into $20.

Of course, we had some costs with the paint and the wheel, along with some elbow grease. The return was still good, and Brayden walked away learning how to invest! This is a simple example of how you can personally invest. You can put that money into a business venture, renovating and reselling items, or learning how to invest stocks yourself.

Before you invest, have some money tucked away in an emergency fund. I recommend starting around $1,000, and then building your emergency fund and investments simultaneously until you feel comfortable with the amount you have saved. When you're just getting started, a portion of your investment budget might go toward saving for a down payment on your first home.

When you learn to how to create and stick to a budget that works for you, you are becoming a master of your money. It's going to be difficult to set aside the funds at first, especially when you're used to spending that money. Through the process of budgeting, you will learn the self-control and discipline necessary to build and retain wealth.

Step 3: Know the difference between assets and liabilities.

A critical part of managing a budget wisely is knowing the difference between assets and liabilities. For example, when you buy a flat screen TV or a nice sports car, what happens to the value of that item when you take it out of the store? Its value depreciates immediately! It immediately becomes worth less than what you paid for it. These objects are liabilities.

Here's what's amazing to me. People will walk into an electronics store and think nothing of putting $2,000 on credit to buy a smart TV. But when I challenge them to put $5,000 to $6,000 down to buy a $150,000 house, they say, "I'm not going to get in debt." Yet, they think nothing of buying a sports car on credit—even though the moment they drive it off the lot, its value depreciates. And the minute they walk out of the store carrying that ginormous TV and put in the back of their pickup, its value depreciates as well.

When I was younger, we didn't have flat screen TVs—we had monster TVs. I mean, you about had to have a crane to carry one. The first time I bought a TV for our family, I bought it on credit, and I remember I paid right around $450. So here I was, proudly trying to get this $450 gigantic boat anchor that we call a TV into the trunk of my car—all the while not realizing that its value was depreciating with every passing second. It was a liability—an expense that does not pay you back.

Assets, however, are completely different. They are things like stocks, real estate, or businesses. Assets actually bring money to you. The idea is that as the assets bring you money, and then you can send that money out to your expenses and liabilities. There's nothing wrong with buying an engagement ring or a TV or a sports car. But what if you bought it with cash from assets instead of buying it on credit?

When you work on building the Second X, you reach a place of having income from assets. This is the cash you could be spending on liabilities. A liability is money that is paid to someone else; an asset is money that is paid to you. You have to eat food to be able to exist and live, but food is a big expense. There are other needs like this in our lives that are big expenses. We need certain things. The issue, most of the time, is not that something costs too much. The issue is that you can't afford it!

Listen to me. Nobody makes wise financial decisions all the time. I didn't! But if you invest in yourself, you become wiser as you get older. When you do fail, you realize you are learning. You call it *noble failure* instead of *just plain failure*, and you move forward. Your next decision will be better, as will the next one after that.

When you do fail, you realize you are learning. You call it ***noble failure*** instead of ***just plain failure***, and you move forward.

The Net Worth Game

Net worth is the value of the assets a person owns minus the liabilities they owe. Wall Street uses the term *arbitrage* a lot, which, in a general sense, means the knowledge of how to buy assets for less than they're worth. This is what you do when you play the net worth game. For instance, let's say you look at a piece of real estate and you know the property is worth $100,000. However, you know you can buy it for $70,000. When you do this, you increase your asset line and make an instant profit of $30,000. If you borrow $70,000, you will have a total investment of $70,000, but the home is still worth $100,000 by comparable sales. So, you just increased your asset line by another $100,000, but you increased your net worth by $30,000 (take the $70,000 off). It's a bit of a game, but it's an enjoyable one if played properly!

In the Triple-X Factor, assets are represented by the stars and the triangles. Those lines represent the assets you hold as well as the income that comes from those assets. The longer you play the net worth game, the more your passive income accelerates until you are financially free.

Step 4: Eliminate debt.

Consumer debt is one of the biggest plagues to western nations because of how easy it is to access. Student loans, credit card debt, mortgages, and auto loans are all examples of consumer debt that can really hinder one's wealth building process. The good news is that that there are several systems you can use to manage consumer debt effectively.

Let's look at a story about Person One and Person Two to illustrate the most fiscally responsible way to handle consumer debt. Person One earns $54,000 a year. She's lived in her home for five and a half years. She has paid off all of her mortgage, cars, and credit cards in six years. (It is possible for most people to pay off all their debt, including their home mortgage, in seven years by applying all of the principles listed below. Some can even do this in as little as five years if their income line is high.)

After Person One is debt free, she invests the $2,500 a month she allocated toward debt payments in the past. At that rate, twenty-four and a half years later she could own her own home, have no debt, and have $3,200,000 in investments at a ten percent average annual return. She's doing alright for herself!

Now, let's take a look at Person Two. He also earns $54,000 a year. He's lived in his home for five and a half years, but he continues to create debt as he pays it off. He makes his debt payments on time and pays his mortgage out over several decades using standard payments. Twenty-four and a half years later, Person Two owns their own home, but still has other consumer debts. Because they didn't invest, they lost out on the $3 million-plus that Person One earned.

This exemplifies how powerful getting out of debt can be. By simply reversing the direction of your money and investing it instead of spending it, you can end up in a really healthy place down the road. Yet, in America, we're taught how to be consumers. The word *consume* literally means "to destroy." When unchecked, consumerism destroys our power to get wealth. For example, if you purchase a $2,000 TV with a typical credit card, it will take 31 years and 2 months to pay off the balance by making the minimum payment. Read the fine print. You will end up paying a total of $10,202 for a $2,000 TV with the average credit card interest rate. That's $8,202 in interest alone! Technology moves so quickly that the TV won't be worth hardly anything by the time it's paid off.

For a more aggressive illustration, let's take a look at a conservative mortgage. Say there's a $275,000 property with a 30-year mortgage at a 5 percent interest rate. When these numbers are run through an amortization schedule (a table of periodic loan payments that shows the amount of principal and the amount of interest that comprise each payment until the loan is paid off at the end of its term), it reveals that a $275,000 mortgage would end up costing $531,453 by the time it's paid off. That's $256,453 in interest!

In 1982, I read *The Richest Man in Babylon* by George S. Clason. It's a powerful book that offers a great basic understanding of finance. Clason makes the point that you can spend 70 percent of what you make on anything you want if you properly manage the remaining 30 percent. In other words, it is okay to purchase whatever you want as long as you're doing it within 80 percent or 70 percent of your income and investing the rest well. That 80 percent is meant to cover your liabilities. Listening to Clason's advice, however, is even better. If you learn to live on the 80 percent and start building passive income, don't start buying real toys until you can pay for them from your passive income. With a just a little patience, you'll be in a place of financial freedom.

In 2020, outstanding consumer debt in the U.S. reached $14.88 trillion, according to data from an Experian consumer debt study.[2] Debt is oppressive and can add up quickly. Whether it's student loans, credit card debt, your mortgage, or a combination of all three, you can stop your debt from snowballing and roll it the other way by sticking to the nine steps in the next chapter.

NOTES

1. Robert Lindsey, "Opening of Glass Cathedral is a Feast for Eyes and Ears," *The New York Times*, May 1980, A20.

2. Nicolas Vega, "Here's how much debt Americans have at every age," CNBC.com, October 13, 2021, https://www.cnbc.com/2021/10/13/how-much-debt-each-generation-has-in-the-us.html.

CHAPTER 5

NINE STEPS
TO GET OUT OF DEBT

Getting out of debt is the foundation for building wealth, but it requires dedication. Therefore, your motivation must be strong. Answer these questions to identify and solidify your goals: Why do you want to be debt-free? What is the main thing that keeps you in debt? What is your winning percentage? How will freedom from debt impact your dream? For instance, my motive to build wealth stems from a desire for a platform to positively change the world. I also want to do everything in my power to help my family to walk in the blessings of God. Continually remind yourself of your "why." It will give you the strength to stick to your debt elimination plan. With that, here's how to get out of debt in nine steps.

STEP 1: CUT UP OR FREEZE ALL BUT ONE CREDIT CARD.

Break out the scissors and destroy those credit cards. Typically, people only need to carry one card when they're trying to eliminate credit card debt. Your spending habits will dictate how strict you need to be. Some people literally need to get a metal coffee can, fill it with water, place their cards into the can, and stick it in their freezer! (It needs to be a metal can so you can't dethaw the card quickly in a microwave.) By the time the water has melted, hopefully the desire to use the credit card for an impulsive purchase will have passed. Find out a method that helps you evaluate your spending decisions and mitigates impulse purchases.

Once you get your system in place, your days of burying yourself in debt will be over! However, don't cancel your credit card accounts. This will have a significant negative impact on your credit score. Instead, stop using the accounts and pay them off. This will improve your score!

~~~~~~~~~~~~~~~~~~~~~~~

However, don't cancel your credit card accounts. This will have a significant negative impact on your credit score.

~~~~~~~~~~~~~~~~~~~~~~~

STEP 2: PAY OFF CURRENT CHARGES EVERY MONTH OR STOP USING THE CARD ALTOGETHER.

If you decide not to freeze your remaining credit card, you need to get serious about how you handle it. Pay off the current charges each month (or, even better, switch to a debit card). The key here is to religiously pay off the card. If you charge $200, then you need to commit to pay $200—not $10 at the end of the month. Even though credit cards give you the option to pay the minimum, paying the balance prevents interest from accruing. The following steps will be difficult if you don't maintain this step. You need to prevent further debt as you eliminate your backlog of previous debt.

STEP 3: MAKE THE MINIMUM PAYMENT ON ALL DEBTS.

Don't be sporadic when you attack debt. Start a rhythm. Further along, I'll show you how to accelerate your plan of attack. But for now, let's establish a base.

Make the minimum payments regularly on all your debts. Note that this is different than your current credit card balance. That needs to be paid off in full each month. However, if you have credit card debt from the past, you need to at least pay the minimum payment each month. It might take a little while to get into this rhythm, but it's the foundation for debt elimination (and crucial for a good credit score). After this step, you can begin to accelerate your debt elimination process.

STEP 4: LIST YOUR CURRENT DEBTS.

List your mortgage, car debt, credit card debt, school loans, and other debts you may have on a spreadsheet. List the debt, the balance, and your current monthly payment (without the taxes and insurance). We just want to look at the hard numbers here. Next, divide the minimum monthly payment into the balance to find the number of months it would take to pay off each debt. Check out the example below of what it might look like when you're done.

List Your Current Debts

DEBT	BALANCE	PAYMENT	# OF MONTHS
Mortgage @ 6%	$139,000	$899.33	154
Car	$7,800	$522.65	14
Car 2	$21,500	$457.12	47
Credit Card 1	$2,250	$55.60	40
Credit Card 2	$1,850	$37.00	50
Home Equity	$18,700	$272.66	68

STEP 5: BEGIN WITH THE DEBT PAID OFF THE QUICKEST USING THE MINIMUM MONTHLY PAYMENT.

The key to debt reduction is to attack the debt that can be paid off the quickest first, not the one with the highest interest rate. Most people start with the debt that has the highest interest, and because of that, they never seem to get ahead. It's more effective to start with the debt that can be paid off in the shortest number of months. According to our sample debt list, that would be starting with Car 1. So, tackle this debt with some oomph!

Back in our younger days, Becky sat down with a yellow legal pad and wrote out all of our expenses and debts (she's the money manager in our relationship). We had never heard of this debt elimination plan before, but through her intuition, Becky followed steps three through five. What we were able to accomplish was amazing. In nearly 11 months, we paid off everything we owed except our mortgage. This principle allowed us to pay down our debt in an incredibly short period of time, and it can help you, too!

The key to debt reduction is to attack the debt that can be paid off the quickest first, not the one with the highest interest rate.

STEP 6: DETERMINE YOUR WINNING PERCENTAGE.

Your winning percentage is the secret sauce to destroying your debt quickly. Your winning percentage is the extra room you have in your budget. In the next step, you'll allocate that extra amount toward your debt payments. After you list all your expenses like Step 5 instructed, you'll be aware of how much money is left over in your budget after all your expenses are paid.

Your winning percentage is the secret sauce to destroying your debt quickly.

As mentioned in the previous chapter, living on 70 to 80 percent of your income is a great practice to begin (meaning that you cover all your expenses within that percentage). Ideally, according to the model we've discussed, living on 80 percent would mean that you tithe 10 percent and invest 10 percent. But for people in heavy debt, it would be better to take the 10 percent you would normally invest and use those funds as your winning percentage to get out of debt. So, in this scenario, you would tithe 10 percent and use 10 percent to get out of debt.

If you live off 70 percent, then invest 10 percent, tithe 10 percent, and keep 10 percent as your winning percentage to pay off debt. To reiterate, a winning percentage is the percent of your income that is not currently used by your budget. If you need 100 percent of your income to pay your expenses, continue to dig around in your budget until you find anything extra to put toward debt elimination.

Here are some questions to help you create a larger winning percentage. These questions are not the most fun to answer, but as we said earlier, it's important to locate where you are so you know how to move ahead.

- What can I sell?

- What expenses can I reduce or eliminate from my life?
- How can I earn extra money?

Getting out of debt is like digging trenches—it's hard work, but when the work is done, the waters can flow.

STEP 7: APPLY YOUR WINNING PERCENTAGE TO THE DEBT THAT CAN BE PAID OFF THE QUICKEST.

In the example from the previous chart, the debt that can be paid off the quickest is Car 1. It can be paid off in 14 months with the minimum monthly payment. Now, let's say our winning percentage is 10 percent of our combined monthly income (or $540), and add it to the minimum payment of $522. Suddenly, you have an accelerated payment of over $1,000 a month. This accelerates the time frame to seven months. So, now you can pay off this debt in half the amount of time!

STEP 8: ONCE A DEBT IS PAID OFF, APPLY ITS TOTAL MONTHLY PAYMENT TO THE NEXT DEBT.

Now the snowball is really rolling! Since the first debt is completely paid off, apply the total you were paying on the first debt—winning percentage included—to the debt that can be paid of the next quickest. Here's where we start cooking with grease, so to speak.

Car 1

MONTHLY PAYMENT	$522.65
Winning percentage	$540.00
New Accelerated Payment	$1062.65
New # of Months	7
Old # of Months	14

Continuing with this example, you would take the accelerated payment from Car 1 and apply it to the next shortest debt: Credit Card 1. Credit Card 1's monthly minimum is $55.60, but once we add the payment of $1,062.65 from Car 1, our total accelerated payment will be $1,118.25 per month. Now, we can pay Credit Card 1 off in less than two months. Instead of the snowball rolling you over, you're pushing it!

Again, when that debt (Credit Card 1) is paid off, you will take the total accelerated payment ($1,118.25) and apply it to the minimum monthly payment of the next shortest debt—Car 2. Add $1,118.25 to Car 2's minimum payment of $457.12 to get a payment of $1,575.37 per month. Now, Car 2 can be paid off in just over a year instead of four years! Repeat this pattern until you are debt free.

The numbers we're using here are real numbers. Using this example, I got completely out of debt, including my mortgage, in 84 months (or seven years). You can too!

STEP 9: APPLY YOUR VASTLY INCREASING WINNING PERCENTAGE TO ACCUMULATING ASSETS.

By this point, you will have a huge winning percentage that you can distribute into accumulating assets. The time has come to move toward the Second X. After you complete these steps, take all of the "free money" you have lying around and put it toward something. Begin to build your investment or passive income—Second-X income—by taking those funds and converting them to investments such as real estate, business, and stocks. *Build wealth!*

Debt elimination is the first step to building wealth.

DEBT	BALANCE	ACCELERATED PAYMENT	# OF MONTHS
Car 1	$7,800	$1,062.65	7
Credit Card 1	$2,258	$1,118.25	2
Car 2	$21,500	$1,575.37	14
Credit Card 2	$1,850	$1,612.37	2
Home Equity	$18,700	$1,885.03	10
Mortgage	$139,000	$2,784.36	49
TOTAL			84

Debt elimination is the first step to building wealth. Many people think that getting out of debt is the end of the road. They believe they have nowhere else to go and nothing else to learn. But, friend, that's not the end. After you erase your debt, you have a new threshold. You are positioned to build serious wealth. Don't stop now! Continue full speed ahead by acquiring assets, building wealth, and playing the net worth game. Work hard on the First X, and from there it's onward and upward. Position yourself to build wealth in the Second X. God has money out there with your name on it. In fact, He says there are hidden riches waiting for you in secret places.

> I will give you the treasures of darkness and hidden riches of secret places, that you may know that I, the Lord, who call you by your name, am the God of Israel (Isaiah 45:3).

As we dive deeper on this on the topic of wealth building, I will reveal some nuances, or what I like to call "secret sauce," to finding these riches that God has for us. There is no reason why the wicked should have the most financial influence in the world. I found the money with my name on it, and now I'm at a place where I can give it away. I want to help you reach that place also.

It's time for the Body of Christ to let the eyes of our understanding be enlightened. Then we will be able to see, understand, and know that we can walk *God's Road to Financial Freedom*. God wants us to be blessed so that we can be a blessing!

SUMMARY

For most people, reaching the First X is their starting goal in the Triple-X Factor, and there are four steps to reach it.

Step 1: Become more valuable.

1. Learn through reading and going through financial programs.

2. Listen by finding a mentor and knowledgeable friends.

3. Look by observing and questioning how people became successful. Success leaves clues.

Step 2: Learn to live on 80 percent.

With 80 percent going to your expenses—debts, rent, food, fun, etc.—tithe 10 percent, have 5 percent professionally invested, and personally invest the other 5 percent.

Step 3: Know the difference between assets and liabilities.

Liabilities—items like cars, jewelry, and TVs—depreciate after you buy them and are worth even less later. Assets like real estate, stocks, and businesses appreciate after you buy them and are worth even more later.

Step 4: Building the First X: Eliminate debt.

We looked at nine steps to get out of debt:

1. Cut up or freeze all but one credit card.
2. Pay off credit charges monthly or quit using the card altogether.
3. Make the minimum payment on all debts.
4. List your current debts.
5. Begin with the debt paid off the quickest using minimum monthly payment.
6. Determine your winning percentage.
7. Apply your winning percentage to the debt paid off the next quickest.

GOD'S ROAD TO FINANCIAL FREEDOM

8. Once a debt is paid off, apply its monthly payment to the next debt.

9. Apply your vastly increasing winning percentage to accumulating assets. Best yet, eliminating debt sets you up to build wealth!

God has money out there with your name on it! Isaiah 45:3 says, "I will give you the treasures of darkness and hidden riches of secret places, that you may know that I, the Lord, who call you by your name, am the God of Israel." God wants you to find these "hidden riches" so you can be blessed and be a blessing!

CHAPTER 6

THE SECOND X:
BUILDING WEALTH

With perseverance and patience, soon your income line and your expense line will cross. In other words, you will have more income than expenses! This is where the wealth ball really starts rolling. When you are armed with excess, you can begin to invest aggressively. You will be able to reach your goal, financial freedom, much more quickly from this point.

Second-X income—or asset income—comes from positive cash flow received from marketable assets that increase in value over time. In other words, it's passive income. Building wealth, in this instance, looks like creating and accumulating assets. If they are true assets, they should grow in value, thus increasing your Second-X income.

An example of this would be someone who gets a job right out of college. As the individual gets older, his or her income will increase because he or she gains more knowledge and experience. The employee gets paid for the increase because he or she carries more value to the marketplace. Properly managed assets do the same thing.

After some time, dedication, and application of the four steps we discussed in the previous chapter, you will create the First X. You will start to have a gap between your expenses and income. Then you can take that excess capital and move it to start building the Second X. You do this by investing the extra room in your budget into assets. Then you will gain more assets, and your assets will increase in value. That's how your wealth grows!

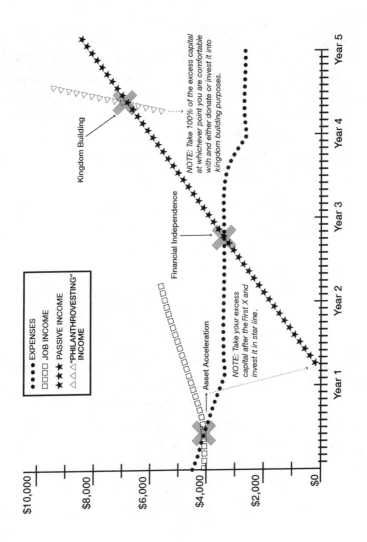

EXPENSES
JOB INCOME
PASSIVE INCOME
"PHILANTHROVESTING" INCOME

Kingdom Building

NOTE: Take 100% of the excess capital at whichever point you are comfortable with and either donate or invest it into kingdom building purposes.

Financial Independence

Asset Acceleration

NOTE: Take your excess capital after the First X and invest it in star line.

$10,000
$8,000
$6,000
$4,000
$2,000
$0

Year 1   Year 2   Year 3   Year 4   Year 5

To reiterate, true assets include rent from real estate, profits from a business, capital distributions from a business, dividends from stocks, royalties from songs and books, interest from bonds, interest from CDs, etc. (For the record, when you buy bonds and CDs, there will be a certain interest rate that is paid. This is called fixed income.) These are the primary areas of income-producing assets.

I recommend buying and holding a rental property and collecting rent from tenants. In my opinion, this form of investing has a low barrier to entry and is relatively risk free. Other places to start are through paid advertisements on your blog or YouTube channel, commissions from insurance, and income from multi-level marketing.

Wealth building is fairly simple—it's just not easy. It takes a lot of energy and effort. You must build the First X, meaning that you have more income than expenses, before you can really start building wealth with assets. Mellody Hobson, as profiled in *Money Magazine*, summed this idea up well by saying: "When I was 22, a friend who is very successful explained to me that no one ever got rich through earned income.

'Look at all the great wealthy families,' he said. 'From Carnegie to Rockefeller, it was never how much they made at work that made them wealthy—it was their investments.' That made me shift from thinking about a paycheck to thinking about building equity and long-term wealth, and it has helped me a lot. Instead of a raise, I ask for more stock."[1]

Wealth building is fairly simple—it's just not easy.

THE RIGHT ATTITUDES

Your attitudes in life can make you or break you. Wrong attitudes prevent you from making the changes you want and need in your life. They hinder relationships. They hinder your ability to make progress on your job. In fact, wrong attitudes hinder you in every area of life and drag you toward defeat just as the right attitudes will propel you toward success. It's no different in the financial realm. Building the Second X requires the right attitudes.

Your attitudes in life can make you or break you.

An attitude is your mindset—what you believe about something deep inside. Your attitudes are determined by your belief system, and what you believe about something will determine how you feel about it. Essentially, attitudes determine how we approach everything in life.

For example, when my kids would come home from college, they would talk to me about problems they were having in their social lives or with their self-esteem. I would always tell them, "I see you need an attitude adjustment." Then I would talk to them about why they believe what they believe. I wanted to help them change how they were feeling about certain situations, and the only way to accomplish that was to help them identify their wrong beliefs about those situations. As soon as they changed their beliefs, their attitudes would swiftly change as well.

If you focus on developing correct attitudes, you will enjoy greater levels of success in developing the Second X.

1. Accept Personal Responsibility

If you've ever caught children doing something wrong, you know their number one tendency is to shift the blame. If you catch them with their hands in the cookie jar, they will try to blame someone else. They might even blame you for making such good cookies! The truth be told, many adults also suffer from this blame-shifting syndrome.

Unfortunately, many people lose interest in personal transformation when they find out they are responsible for making it happen. Sometimes it's easiest to see a principle like this out of context, so let me explain the importance of change in the context of marriage.

When a couple experiences conflict in their marriage, each spouse wants the other to change. However, they aren't willing to change their own behaviors. Wherever you want to see change, change is your responsibility. People try to blame everyone and everything for their problems, but the truth is, in your circumstances, you are the agent of change. This is especially true in the realm of eliminating debt and building wealth. For your financial picture to change, you must change it!

Accepting personal responsibility is the highest form of human maturity. You cannot control everything that happens to you, but you can always control your reaction and your response. For instance, you cannot control the fact that a tornado tore down your house, but you can control what you do about it.

In Mark 9, the Bible tells the story of a father with a sick child. The father asked Jesus if there was anything He could do. Jesus answered him and said, "If you can believe, all things are possible to him who believes" (Mark 9:23). Jesus put the responsibility for health on the father. That may seem unfair, but it effectively illustrates the vital part you play in changing the condition of your own life. You cannot remove yourself from the change equation. Let's put it this way. You are responsible for the *natural*, and God is responsible for the *super*. Together, you have all the *supernatural* help needed to change your circumstances.

Here's yet another scenario where we see the importance of doing everything you can to bring about change in difficult situations—teenagers. Being a parent to teenagers is difficult, and it's easy to tell yourself, "I don't have any influence. I can't control what my teenagers do when they're not in my presence." Maybe not, but you can make creative decisions about how you deal with their actions, provide appropriate consequences, and get outside help if necessary.

As you choose these appropriate responses, your teen's behavior will begin to turn slowly, like a large ship, in the direction you desire it to go. You may not be able to change the *destination* at the moment, but you certainly can change the *direction*. If you cannot change things inside the boat, at least you can influence the direction the boat is heading!

For example, a minister discovered that his teenager was experimenting with drugs. He attempted to talk with his son but could not get through to him. The minister was at the end of his rope. He spent some time alone, praying, and asking God what to do. A drastic answer came to his mind. He would take a leave of absence from his church and do whatever was necessary to reach his boy.

The minister decided to change their environment. He had been totally caught up in the environment of his church, and his son had been totally caught up in the environment of his drug-using friends. So the father made a dramatic decision to take his son on a shrimp boat that remained at sea for three months. This way, neither he nor his son could leave the company of one another.

The results were staggering! By changing their environment, the minister and his son reconnected without any outside interference. The son later said when his father took a leave of absence, he knew his father loved him unconditionally.

I spoke with this minister before and after the trip, and it was apparent that he took complete responsibility for his son's problem. Yes, the son had to choose to change, but it was the father's actions and attitude of personal responsibility that encouraged the son's positive choice.

When you determine to swim upstream rather than be tossed to and fro by the currents of life, you assume responsibility for reaching your destination.

Some of life's most important decisions require some upstream swimming. Ultimately, you are responsible for your direction and destination in life, regardless of opposition.

Accepting personal responsibility also entails giving up all your excuses. Some people go through their entire lives blaming others. They say, "I drink because my dad treated me badly when I was a kid." That may be true, and he may have been a very negative influence on you. "I'm poor because my parents didn't teach me how to manage money." That's unfortunate. But now you are a grown person with the power to choose. You must accept responsibility and quit allowing yourself to play the victim. Personal responsibility is the key for any major change to take place in your life and in your financial picture.

You may not be able to change the destination of your money at this very moment, but you certainly can change the direction. Don't blame someone else for your financial situation. You have the power to choose what happens next. By accepting personal responsibility, you've taken hold of the steering wheel that can drive you success.

> You may not be able to change the destination of your money at this very moment, but you certainly can change the direction.

2. Take Personal Control

Once you've accepted responsibility, it's time to take control. You have the choice to be an active participant in your life. After all, God gave us free will, so we are empowered us to take personal control (while using biblical discretion and listening to the Holy Spirit, of course!).

We all have seen teenagers try to model themselves after someone else. Most teenagers say they want to do their own thing, yet they end up doing the same thing as the rest of their peers. They are heavily influenced by someone else's perception of cool. This this also applies to many adults. Even as adults, we never stop being influenced by someone else's standards. We are still continually bombarded with messages to be, think, or look a certain way. No one lives in a vacuum. Outside influences perpetually try to mold us. For instance, our society tries to convince us that credit card debt is normal, gold credit cards are a status symbol, overspending on shopping sprees is fun. And hey, you get three percent back!

You must take personal control of your life and refuse to be ruled by somebody else's opinion. Miracles can happen when a person makes the decision to stand up and say, "No, I'm not going along with the crowd. I'm going to do things differently." Against all odds, that person will succeed!

Your experiences in life are determined by your choices. If you fall into bankruptcy, you can choose whether or not to accept it. It may not be easy; it may not be automatic. And it will definitely not be without a fight! But you can choose. You have a right to make these choices, and you have more control than you think!

3. Expect the Best

The next attitude necessary for success is to expect the best. Expecting the best is as simple as deciding to see your future in a positive light. Are you expecting the best? What are your expectations concerning wealth? Are they negative or positive? It's important to ask and answer these questions because they show where your faith is. Hebrews 11:1 says, "Now faith is confidence in what we hope for and assurance about what we do not see" (NIV). Trust in God is developed when you expect the best despite your circumstance. You create space for His favor and faithfulness!

Some people constantly look for every negative, disabling event that can possibly happen, and they find them. But, like the apostle Paul wrote in Hebrews, we should have confidence in the hopes that God has placed inside of us. The Bible challenges us to expect the best, work for the best, and have faith for the best.

Another aspect of expecting the best is anticipation. Anticipation is the opposite of apathy, and you can intentionally create it in your routine. Even if it's as simple as treating yourself to a cup of coffee once a week, have something to look forward to! Anticipation makes it to where budgeting and building wealth doesn't feel like a burden. You can strategically position short-term satisfaction (within margin) as you work toward your long-term financial goals.

The Bible challenges us to expect the best, work for the best, and have faith for the best.

The Power of Imagination

In the Nazi concentration camps of World War II, when the Germans were killing Jews by the millions, a professor by the name of Viktor Frankl witnessed the atrocities firsthand. In writing about his experiences, Frankl said one thing that enabled him to endure such horror was he could imagine himself someday teaching again. In his mind, he saw himself standing at the podium lecturing and a classroom of students listening and learning.

He knew escape was not probable, yet the pictures in his imagination gave him something to anticipate. He began to expect the best for his life, and it galvanized his determination to live. Eventually, he made it back into the classroom, and later he wrote the classic book *Man's Search for Meaning*. He shared in the book how from the terrible ordeal he endured to creatively expect the best and, thereby, prevail.

Most people don't expect the best because they have been disappointed too often. However, disappointing things happen to everyone, and we cannot allow those things to paralyze us. We must keep expecting the best so we can prevail.

I like to have three or four things that I am expecting the best about at any given time. I expect the best with my family. I expect the best with my businesses. And I expect the best with my finances. I always write down my expectations so I will have something to be excited about at all times.

When my friend was diagnosed with cancer, I encouraged him to start expecting the best by visualizing himself doing something he really loved. For him, that was bicycle touring. He enjoyed high-tech bikes that were sleek and expensive. In fact, my friend and his doctor found a point of connection over the sport. As they began to discuss specific types of bicycles and upcoming tours, the focus shifted from his illness to something that excited him. He began to look forward to the day he would ride again in certain tours.

When a doctor says, "You have cancer, and now I'm going to give you every gory detail," your focus must be on something positive. Doctors do that because they don't want you to live in denial, but expecting the best is very different from living in denial.

My friend did not deny that he had cancer; he just chose not to focus on it. Instead, he built a mental image of what it would be like to tour again. He built an image of life and hope for his future. It changed his focus and, once he was better, he participated in several bike tours.

Allow me to suggest a few more questions you should ponder to help you expect the best: What images do you presently concentrate on in your mind? What images motivate you to expect the best? What choices are you intentionally making to ensure your present attitude will empower you, not defeat you?

Take whatever measures necessary to change your present attitude to an attitude that allows you to excel. When you see positive results, you will be glad you did!

4. Be Creative

You must be willing to be creative to reach your goals. Maybe you feel stuck or trapped in your current financial situation. Maybe you have some bad habits that you have never been able to break. Or perhaps you think, *I'm never going to change.* No matter where you are right now, if you're creative about it, there is a strategy that will enable you to move forward.

Actually, being creative is one of the most God-like things you can do. God is the ultimate Creator. He sat on the edge of nothingness and told the light, planets, sun, and moon to exist, and then He lit them up. He had a blueprint of what He wanted this universe to look like, and He spoke out what He saw. God has also given you an imagination like His so you can speak out the things you desire for your life.

Actually, being creative is one of the most God-like things you can do.

History is filled with people who dared to imagine physical things that had never existed before. These dreamers and inventors were mocked by those who declared their ideas impossible. Yet, many of those ideas have become the inventions we enjoy today such as the light bulb and the telephone. They only became realities because dreamers were willing to exercise their imaginations.

People have a strong tendency to doubt their own creativity, especially when they need to imagine a way out of their current situation. But God always provides a way for you to get where you need to go. When you really believe there's a way for you to create the changes you desire, you will become creative.

My mother was a stubborn woman. Throughout her entire life, she resisted being pressed into someone else's mold. She faced many health challenges and often refused to respond in the manner doctors thought she should. But hey, she was creative! If the doctors told her she could not walk, she walked. If they told her she could not get out of bed, she got out of bed. I'm not telling you to be irresponsible; I'm merely pointing out that nothing can confine you to your present circumstances if you are willing to be creative and partner with God.

5. Design Your Future

To design your future, you must identify your priorities by determining what is meaningful to you. When you identify your core values and goals, designing your future flows naturally. Be confident and willing to pick up the pen. Then, compose an ending to your own story.

When is the last time you asked yourself "What is important to me?" Too many of us live our lives for someone else, but to successfully design your future, you cannot be limited to what other people think about you or desire for you. If you try to build wealth according to someone else's standards, the change probably won't last. You must choose your own changes for your own reasons and get after them!

It's also important for you to identify your purpose. On one occasion, the CFO of a company asked me how he could find his purpose in life during a financial seminar I was teaching. I told him that his purpose would be revealed when he identified what he desired in life and gave specific direction to those desires. Your purpose is your identified values expressed through your written goals.

When some people try to define their purpose, they do not consider their core values. They usually only think of two groups of surface desires. The first group they consider is what will deliver them from their immediate problems, and the second group they consider is primarily related to money. Even though these desires are significant, people rarely go beyond these surface desires to reach their core values unless they are prodded to do so. So, prod yourself! You must discover your ultimate goal in building wealth before you can truly build wealth. To help determine what is most significant to you, ask yourself these questions: What would I do with my life if money were not an issue? What do I want my tombstone to say about me? What am I doing with my life that will live on after I die?

You must discover your ultimate goal in building wealth before you can truly build wealth.

You see, your purpose becomes your strongest incentive to make necessary changes in your life. Your purpose is like your physical appetite, except it functions on a spiritual level. Your appetite moves you effortlessly toward food, just as your purpose moves you toward the changes you need to make to fulfill your potential. When you meet resistance, your purpose will push you forward.

To have confidence in designing your future, your next step must be to ask for the things you desire. This may sound simplistic, but many dreams have gone unfulfilled because someone failed to ask. The

Bible talks to us about this very thing and tells us that if we ask, we will receive (see Matt. 7:8). That is a powerful and simple formula, but many Christians still go through their life without asking.

One of the best ways to ask is to write out everything you want as precisely as you can. Goals are like targets; precision tells you where to shoot. Most people, however, take the shotgun approach when it comes to getting what they want out of life. They just randomly shoot and hope they hit something. Unfortunately, the results are often as scattered as the shot.

As a youngster, I discovered it was easy to shoot a shotgun and miss! During one afternoon of dove hunting with friends, I shot two boxes of shells before I ever hit a bird. Doves fly fast, and your aim has to be precise to hit one. The same thing is true about your goals; you have to define them precisely if you want to hit your target.

Remember—after you define your goals and ask God for success, you must also have faith that you can obtain your desires. The Bible says it this way:

> *Whatever things you ask when you pray, believe that you receive them, and you will have them* (Mark 11:24).

In other words, you must believe that you are in possession of your goals before you obtain them. You do this by using your sixth sense—faith. For instance, have you ever been desperately thirsty and gulped down a bottle of ice-cold mineral water? If so, you have some idea of how faith works. The sensations you experienced when you drank that water were incredible. The refreshment you felt was unbelievable. Your sense of touch and taste became incredibly alive.

Faith works the same way, except it operates in the spiritual dimension. Faith causes you to experience the sensations of having obtained your desires before you reach them. The sensations of faith are so real that you feel like you are already in possession of your goals before you even reach them. As a matter of fact, when you do reach them, it is no big deal because you have already been experiencing what it is like to have them! You can apply this principle of faith to any desired change. When you experience the sensations of change before it happens, you believe your personal transformation is possible regardless of the obstacles you face.

6. Take Action

Another attitude that is necessary for personal change is the determination to take action. Getting started is half the battle! Many people see what they need to accomplish, think about where they need to go, dream about the possibilities, but then they never move forward. Don't let that be you!

> For as the body without the spirit is dead, so faith without works is dead also (James 2:26).

The actions you take must be harmonious with the outcome you desire. For example, if you say you want to lose weight but keep visiting Dairy Queen, your actions are not in harmony with your desired outcome. As a matter of fact, they are taking you in a direction contrary to where you want to go! You must align your behavior with the change you desire. If you can do this, you will be successful with the growth you choose to undertake.

Your actions toward your goal must also be unwavering! After all, harmonious actions amplify each other, which enable you to become even stronger in the direction you want to pursue. Physical exercise is a good example of a harmonious action, because the more you develop your muscles through continual use, the easier it becomes to do certain exercises. You imprint the desired change into your mind and body by repeating the desired behavior over and over.

Your actions toward your goal must also be unwavering!

For example, have you ever driven to work and forgotten how you got there? If so, it's because the path to your workplace is so entrenched in your mind that you can arrive there with very little conscious thought. Many areas of our lives are the same way. We often find ourselves performing self-defeating behaviors as though we are on autopilot. The good news, however, is that you can imprint positive behaviors on your mind in the same way. The more frequently that you repeat a certain behavior, the more ingrained it will become. Then, over a period of time, the positive behavior will be executed almost subconsciously.

7. Adapt to Succeed

The last attitude you need to develop is a willingness to adapt. There are two ideas you need to grasp to understand this concept: when to adapt your behaviors, and when to adapt to changing cultural times. First off, if you do not enjoy the results you are getting in life, change what you are doing. Someone once defined insanity as doing the same thing over and over again while expecting different results!

If you bounce a ball the same way every time, it will respond accordingly. If you bounce it harder or softer, you will get different results. Likewise, you need to watch the outcomes you get from the actions you take. Then, if you are not obtaining your desired results, you must be willing to change your actions.

Second, it's critical to be flexible during changing times. Some people do not change with the times, so they get left behind. This happened to the railroad companies in the earlier part of the 20th century. They believed they were in the train business instead of the transportation business, and due to this faulty belief, they failed to make the necessary changes that would have allowed them to keep up with the changing times. Personally, I am fascinated with trains, but when I travel from Denver to New York, I take a jet!

Things have changed a lot in the past two decades. The introduction of the internet and e-commerce is drastically changing how we live, shop, work, and play. Companies and individuals who do not adapt to changes like these will get left behind.

Luckily, you are already making progress by examining and developing the attitudes of success. The bottom line is that all of us can either remain stuck or grow. If you do not move forward, you will soon drift backward. If you concentrate on building the seven positive attitudes we have examined in this chapter, you will be ready to face any changes that come your way along your wealth building process.

Hovering over the Face of the Waters

Most people in America are taught how to earn money, save money, and get out of debt. But debt elimination is not the highest point of freedom, and until you are taught how to make money, you won't reach true financial freedom. You need to ask yourself the following questions: Where do I go after I am free from debt? How do I get there? How do I start building the Second X?

You need to adapt your mindset from a focus on earning money to a focus on making money. I am so grateful to be able to provide microfinance loans through Tricord Global because most of our clients in developing countries don't have another way to obtain capital. There are few opportunities for people in the countries we service to get jobs. I'm connected to an American MBA program in Africa, but after students graduate from it, they still can't get a job because there aren't enough jobs to go around. In the United States, it's hard for us to understand that because we are a prosperous nation with lots of employment opportunities. Yet having lots of employment opportunities in America also lends itself to its own set of problems. People tend to keep themselves in a box since they can earn money. In other words, they don't think about making money. On the contrary, in Africa they can really only obtain money through entrepreneurship. However, it's difficult to raise the funds to get started. In other words, they must begin at the Second X (without having developed the skills in the First X!). In a way, they're at an advantage because their circumstance has directed their focus to making money rather than earning it. However, they need a hand up to receive the startup capital, which is where Tricord Global offers their services.

For example, if I gave most people in the United States $1, would they be able to turn it into $2? For most people, the answer is no because they do not know how to build wealth. That's the reason we have such a challenge teaching the Second X in the U.S. I strongly believe in working. I work even though I don't need to, but I do it because God's called me to do so. It's not that work isn't good; work is very good. But wealth building is dependent on making money through passive income generation. Look with me at the scripture below.

> In the beginning God created the heavens and the earth. The earth was without form, and void; and darkness was on the face of the deep. And the Spirit of God was hovering over the face of the waters (**Genesis 1:1-2**).

This process of "hovering" is how God releases the creative process in you. It starts with God leading and guiding you. In this passage, we see that the Holy Spirit was brooding, or hovering, over the face of the waters. Out of that hovering, God said, "Let there be light." And out of that brooding, God began to create the heavens and earth.

How does this apply to you? You must make the time to learn and to think about what God wants you to do next. You must spend time brooding and hovering before you make a move.

As I mentioned earlier, 50 percent of accomplishing anything is taking the first step. Some people say that's too simple. Not at all. If I get my feet in the water, I find that the water often begins to part. That's when God shows up and shows the way. You will begin to move forward in this creative process with Him. But first, you've got to take a step of faith!

Take inventory of yourself. Examine your core competencies, your personality, your motivation, your risk tolerance, your ability to deal with difficult people, etc. Use tools like Myers-Briggs and StrengthsFinder to help you in this process. Whatever personality test or personal inventory guide you choose to use, make sure what you're reading resonates and is applicable. It's important to understand yourself and your limitations, and then to actively deny those limitations the power to prevent you from going where God wants you to go.

You can have an impact and partnership with God in the creative process. If you encounter limitations, always remember that with God all things are possible (see Matt. 19:26). God is not limited by your limitations. If you believe that, you will be able to move to the place God has for you.

If you encounter limitations, always remember that with God all things are possible (see Matt. 19:26). God is not limited by your limitations.

Remember, you take value to the marketplace. So when you're building the Second X, it's very important that you continue to invest in yourself. Building the First X can be done in a series of steps, but building the Second X and Third X is not quite as straight of a shot. Instead, there are many different routes and tools to building wealth at this level. While you may not be able to envision exactly what the path looks like going forward, you can trust God and sound financial wisdom to direct the way.

I can't tell you exactly how God will build wealth in your life. It may be through real estate like it was for me. Or, it may be through stocks and bonds or business. Only you and the Lord can answer that question. But remember that God allows you time to hover before you jump into a new venture. He gives you time to plan, think, and collect information before you begin taking steps and walking out the plan. As you begin the process of gaining assets, spend time brooding and praying over your motives and your plans. He's given you His Word that He will order you steps (see Ps. 37:23).

SUMMARY

With perseverance and patience, soon your income line and your expense line will cross. In other words, you will have more income than expenses! This is where the wealth ball really starts rolling. When you are armed with excess, you can begin to invest aggressively. You will be able to reach your goal, financial freedom, much more quickly from this point.

Examples of assets: True assets include things like rent from real estate, profits from a business, capital distributions from a business, dividends from stock, royalties from songs and books, interest from bonds, interest from CDs, etc.

Building the Second X requires the right mindset. Having the wrong attitude can hinder you financially because your attitudes make you or break you.

Seven attitudes you need to excel in wealth-building include:

1. Accept personal responsibility
2. Take personal control

3. Expect the best

4. Be creative

5. Have confidence to design your future

6. Take action

7. Adapt to succeed

Most people in America are taught how to earn money, save money, and get out of debt. But debt elimination is not the highest point of freedom, and until you are taught how to make money, you won't reach true financial freedom.

NOTE

1. Mellody Hobson, "The smartest advice I ever got: What I learned from Andrew Carnegie," CNN Money, https://money.cnn.com/galleries/2008/pf/0807/gallery.smartest_advice.moneymag/5.html.

CHAPTER 7

THE THIRD X:
WEALTHY AND WISE

By this final chapter in the book, you have journeyed along *God's Road to Financial Freedom*. You've put in the effort, mastered your money, and built wealth. But where has this road led? What was the purpose of your journey? You have reached the Third X, a place of immense freedom where you are able to direct your wealth any way you want. With great wealth comes great responsibility. *God's Road to Financial Freedom* leads to a place of rich blessings that can be used to bless others. Remember the Abrahamic Covenant from Chapter 2? At this stage, you can fully embrace, cultivate, and serve in the areas that God has brought you to. God has empowered you to succeed and, in turn, you can use your wealth and wisdom to empower others to have a relationship with God and do the same.

Of course, you can give at every X. In fact, you should always be tithing and giving. You don't have to wait to bless and serve until you reach the Third X, but you have arrived at a new dimension. You now release a level of fully owning your options for giving at the Third X. You have a deeper level of ownership and ability at the Third X.

The triangles on your Triple-X chart that indicate the Third X start quite a bit out from where the Second X is formed. This is intentional. This shows that you must have the ability to live off your Second-X income before you can reach the Third-X level of giving 100 percent of your additional passive income away. However, in due time your passive income streams will produce a return that exceeds the amount you need for a satisfactory lifestyle.

At the Third X, you have become an investor who holds assets that yield much fruit for you to enjoy. Your money no longer masters you; instead, it's working for you—without you. But now, you have a big choice to make: What will you do with all your money? Or an even more important question: What is the whole point of financial freedom?

~~~~~~~~~~~~~~~~~~~~

Your money no longer masters you; instead, it's working for you—without you.

~~~~~~~~~~~~~~~~~~~~

ESTABLISHING THE COVENANT

In my own life, my initial motivation to master my money and become financially free was totally for selfish reasons. In the beginning, I didn't think about wealth from a godly perspective. Rather, I wanted to be able to quit my job and not have anyone telling me what to do! It wasn't long before God showed me that He didn't give me the power to get wealth so that I could go play golf every day. When I had that revelation, God showed me that financial freedom was about creating the space to do God's will. In my life, that meant empowering others to find the same financial freedom I had so that they could better serve God.

Look again at this key scripture in Deuteronomy 8:17-18. It's where this book began, and it is where we will come full circle.

> Then you say in your heart, "My power and the might of my hand have gained me this wealth." And you shall remember the Lord your God, for it is He who gives you the pow-

er to get wealth, that He may establish His covenant which He swore to your fathers, as it is this day (Deuteronomy 8:17-18).

God gave the Israelites the power to get wealth so that He could establish the Abrahamic Covenant. Through this covenant, He promised to give them a land and to make them a great nation. This covenant revealed God's love for His people, and it revealed His glory as the one true God. The reason God gives us the power to get wealth isn't all that different. He wants his glory to be revealed through our lives, too. Therefore, our wealth comes with an assignment. We are to use our finances, along with every platform and position we have, unto the glory of God (see 1 Cor. 10:31).

More to the point, you've already proven that you can master your money—that's what got you out of debt and into wealth. Now, you have a responsibility to manage your wealth.

> **God's purpose for wealth is to make a difference.**

MAKING A DIFFERENCE

God's purpose for wealth is to make a difference. We see this principal in the story of the Good Samaritan. I like a quote by former United Kingdom Prime Minister Margaret Thatcher, who said, "Nobody would remember the Good Samaritan if he only had good intentions. He had money as well." That's because he had the financial means to care for the wounded traveler! Check out the passage below:

> *A Jewish man was traveling from Jerusalem down to Jericho, and he was attacked by*

bandits. They stripped him of his clothes, beat him up, and left him half dead beside the road. By chance a priest came along. But when he saw the man lying there, he crossed to the other side of the road and passed him by. A Temple assistant walked over and looked at him lying there, but he also passed by on the other side. Then a despised Samaritan came along, and when he saw the man, he felt compassion for him. Going over to him, the Samaritan soothed his wounds with olive oil and wine and bandaged them. Then he put the man on his own donkey and took him to an inn, where he took care of him. The next day he handed the innkeeper two silver coins, telling him, "Take care of this man. If his bill runs higher than this, I'll pay you the next time I'm here" (Luke 10:30-35 NLT).

If we're not careful, many of us fall into the same category as the Jewish priest or temple assistant. The priest probably had the resources to help the man because of the Jewish belief about wealth as a virtue, but he was so engrossed in his own world that he did not help him. It could be that the temple assistant didn't have any money to even consider helping the injured man, but he should have at least stopped to check on him. Either way, one man was absorbed with his own affairs while the other one had no ability to help.

The Samaritans were despised by the Jews. But evidently, the Good Samaritan did not allow what the Jews thought about him, or Samaritans in general, to stop him from becoming a prosperous, blessed man who operated in the covenant of God. He didn't allow their snootiness or their negative opinions of him and his people bother him in the least.

He said, "Here's enough money to take care of what the man's bill should be. If the bill is higher, when I come back through, I'll take care of it." Since he was coming back through and therefore probably traveled a lot, he was likely some sort of merchant. That's also likely why he had the finances to help the injured man in need. The good Samaritan had the good resources to take a tragic situation and elevate it into something better.

The Jewish priest and the temple assistant didn't do anything. Then came along a despised Samaritan who had resources, compassion, and know-how. Most importantly, he had a heart that was willing to give sacrificially. One of the reasons that God wants us to prosper is so that we can emulate the compassion the Good Samaritan showed through his intentional giving to the needy.

If you are reading this, I pray 3 John 1:2 over your life: "Beloved, I pray that you may prosper in all things." God wants us to prosper so that we can bring Matthew 6:10 to life: "Your Kingdom come. Your will be done on earth as it is in heaven." As we prosper, everyone partners with God to bring His Kingdom to earth in different ways. God's Kingdom is one where the last is first (see Matt. 19:30), leadership means service (see Matt. 20:28), and justice and peace are restored (see Rom. 14:17). So, as you accrue more resources, ask God how He wants you to steward them. Maybe you're meant to financially support a nonprofit that helps restore justice to those who have been through sex trafficking. Maybe you're meant to start a church. Or, maybe you're meant to invest in microfinance business loans to help bring economic equality to people in need. God has placed a unique calling on every one of us!

BIGGER BARNS OR BIGGER PURPOSE

In Luke 12, Jesus told the story of a rich farmer who was focused on building bigger barns. Jesus used this example to teach them—and us—how we should use our wealth. The parable is introduced by a member of the crowd listening to Jesus, who tried to get Jesus to resolve a family financial dispute.

> Then someone called from the crowd, "Teacher, please tell my brother to divide our father's estate with me."
>
> Jesus replied, "Friend, who made me a judge over you to decide such things as that?" Then he said, "Beware! Guard against every kind of greed. Life is not

measured by how much you own" (Luke 12:13-15 NLT).

Jesus continues to make His point and shares the following parable.

> *Then he told them a story: "A rich man had a fertile farm that produced fine crops. He said to himself, 'What should I do? I don't have room for all my crops.' Then he said, 'I know! I'll tear down my barns and build bigger ones. Then I'll have room enough to store all my wheat and other goods. And I'll sit back and say to myself, "My friend, you have enough stored away for years to come. Now take it easy! Eat, drink, and be merry!"' But God said to him, 'You fool! You will die this very night. Then who will get everything you worked for?'"* (Luke 12:16-20 NLT)

Sure, you can use your wealth to build bigger houses and barns, eat, drink, and be merry. But Jesus called this option foolish. In fact, the Jewish mindset sees wealth accumulation as a virtue—but not for the purpose of building bigger barns. God wants you to have barns so you can have an impact in the earth and partner with Him for the Kingdom's cause. The reason God wants you to have barns is not so you can eat, drink, and be merry but so you can make a difference.

I named my nonprofit company WealthBuilders after Deuteronomy 8:18, where we read that God gives us the power and the right to grow wealth. We're not about trying to build something to heap riches on ourselves; we're about advancing the Kingdom of God in the earth.

Let me be clear. God absolutely does want you to live blessed and walk in abundance in every area of life. He wants you to build wealth. He wants you to own barns. But it's not about building bigger barns. It's about prospering in the barns you already have. When it comes time to build bigger barns, that's where we partner with God to follow His plans and purposes for wealth.

One of my greatest blessings has been donating to certain ministries or endeavors, and one of my greatest delights has been helping people overseas by starting nonprofits like Tricord Global and WealthBuilders. Through these organizations, we are able to provide loans and educations to people who really need help.

We're not about trying to build something to heap riches on ourselves; we're about advancing the Kingdom of God in the earth.

God is partnering with you as well. As you seek Him, He will direct you. God gave you the power to get wealth, and God will empower you to be a blessing.

SUMMARY

You have walked *God's Road to Financial Freedom* and arrived at the destination. You've put in the effort, mastered your money, and built wealth. This is the moment when you get to mirror the Abrahamic Covenant and walk into the Promised Land that God has for you.

God's purpose for wealth is to make a difference.

The Good Samaritan didn't just have a kind heart. He had the resources to help in the case of an emergency (see Luke 10:30-35).

God wants you to be abundantly blessed. He wants you to build wealth. But godly wealth is not about building bigger barns. It's about prospering in the barns you already have. When it comes time to build bigger barns, that's when you continue partnering with God for His direction (see Luke 12:16-21).

God has given you the power to get wealth, and He will empower you to be a blessing.

WHAT GOD'S WORD
SAYS ABOUT FINANCES

Then you say in your heart, "My power and the might of my hand have gained me this wealth." And you shall remember the Lord your God, for it is He who gives you the power to get wealth, that He may establish His covenant which He swore to your fathers, as it is this day (Deuteronomy 8:17-18).

And all these blessings shall come on thee, and overtake thee, if thou shalt hearken unto the voice of the Lord thy God (Deuteronomy 28:2 KJV).

The Lord shall open unto thee his good treasure, the heaven to give the rain unto thy land in his season, and to bless all the work of thine hand: and thou shalt lend unto many nations, and thou shalt not borrow (Deuteronomy 28:12 KJV).

Keep therefore the words of this covenant, and do them, that ye may prosper in all that ye do (Deuteronomy 29:9 KJV).

Only be strong and very courageous, that you may observe to do according to all the law which Moses My servant commanded you; do not turn from it to the right hand or to the left, that you may prosper wherever you go. This Book of the Law shall not depart from your mouth, but you shall meditate in it day and night, that you may observe to do according to all that is written in it. For then you will make your way prosperous, and then you will have good success (Joshua 1:7-8).

And he shall be like a tree planted by the rivers of water, that bringeth forth his fruit in his season; his leaf also shall not wither; and whatsoever he doeth shall prosper (Psalm 1:3 KJV).

The Lord is my shepherd; I have everything I need (Psalm 23:1 NLT).

Delight yourself also in the Lord, and He shall give you the desires of your heart. Commit your way to the Lord, trust also in Him, and He shall bring it to pass (Psalm 37:4-5).

The Lord will perfect that which concerns me (Psalm 138:8).

The fear of the Lord is the beginning of knowledge. But fools despise wisdom and instruction (Proverbs 1:7 KJV).

Those who love me inherit wealth. I will fill their treasuries (Proverbs 8:21 NLT).

He who has a slack hand becomes poor, but the hand of the diligent makes rich (Proverbs 10:4).

The blessing of the Lord makes one rich, and He adds no sorrow with it (Proverbs 10:22).

Good people leave an inheritance to their grandchildren, but the sinner's wealth passes to the godly (Proverbs 13:22 NLT).

The reward of humility and the reverent and worshipful fear of the Lord is riches and honor and life (Proverbs 22:4 AMPC).

Through skillful and godly Wisdom is a house (a life, a home, a family) built, and by understanding it is established [on a sound and good foundation], and by knowledge shall its chambers [of every area] be filled with all precious and pleasant riches (Proverbs 24:3-4 AMPC).

Any enterprise is built by wise planning, becomes strong through common sense, and profits wonderfully by keeping abreast of the facts (Proverbs 24:3-4 TLB).

A faithful man will abound with blessings (Proverbs 28:20).

Greed causes fighting; trusting the Lord leads to prosperity (Proverbs 28:25 NLT).

A dull ax requires great strength; be wise and sharpen the blade (Ecclesiastes 10:10 TLB).

If you are willing and obedient, you shall eat the good of the land (Isaiah 1:19).

I will give you the treasures of darkness and hidden riches of secret places, that you may know that I, the Lord, who call you by your name, am the God of Israel (Isaiah 45:3).

My people are destroyed for lack of knowledge (Hosea 4:6).

"Bring all the tithes into the storehouse, that there may be food in My house, and try Me now in this," says the Lord of hosts, "if I will not open for you the windows of heaven and pour out for you such blessing that there will not be room enough to receive it" (Malachi 3:10).

Do not lay up for yourselves treasures on earth, where moth and rust destroy and where thieves break in and steal; but lay up for yourselves treasures in heaven, where neither moth nor rust destroys and where thieves do not break in and steal. For where your treasure is, there your heart will be also (Matthew 6:19-21).

No one can serve two masters, for either he will hate the one and love the other, or he will be devoted to the one and despise the other. You cannot serve God and money (Matthew 6:24 ESV).

For assuredly, I say to you, whoever says to this mountain, "Be removed and be cast into the sea," and does not doubt in his heart, but believes that those things he says will be done, he will have whatever he says. Therefore I say to you, whatever things you ask when you pray, believe that you receive them, and you will have them (Mark 11:23-24).

For you are becoming progressively acquainted with and recognizing more strongly and clearly the grace of our Lord Jesus Christ (His kindness, His gracious generosity, His undeserved favor and spiritual blessing), [in] that though He was [so very] rich, yet for your sakes He became [so very] poor, in order that by His poverty you might become enriched (abundantly supplied) (2 Corinthians 8:9 AMPC).

And God is able to make all grace (every favor and earthly blessing) come to you in abundance, so that you may always and under all circumstances and whatever the need be self-sufficient [possessing enough to require no aid or support and furnished in abundance for every good work and charitable donation] (2 Corinthians 9:8 AMPC).

And my God shall supply all your need according to His riches in glory by Christ Jesus (Philippians 4:19).

For He [God] Himself has said, I will not in any way fail you nor give you up nor leave you without support. [I will] not, [I will] not, [I will] not in any degree leave you helpless nor forsake nor let [you] down (relax My hold on you)! [Assuredly not!] (Hebrews 13:5 AMPC).

If any of you lacks wisdom, let him ask of God, who gives to all liberally and without reproach, and it will be given to him (James 1:5).

Casting the whole of your care [all your anxieties, all your worries, all your concerns, once and for all] on Him, for He cares for you affectionately and cares about you watchfully (1 Peter 5:7 AMPC).

Beloved, I pray that you may prosper in all things and be in health, just as your soul prospers (3 John 2).

ABOUT

BILLY EPPERHART

Billy Epperhart is a successful entrepreneur, investor, and a nationally known speaker and author. He is the CEO of Andrew Wommack Ministries and Charis Bible College, as well as the co-founder of the Charis Business School. In addition, he oversees the strategic direction of his nonprofit, WealthBuilders, which provides financial and spiritual education to help people make sense of making money for making a difference. The missional arm of WealthBuilders, Tricord Global, provides microfinance loans and business training in developing nations.

The Harrison House Vision

Proclaiming the truth and the power
of the Gospel of Jesus Christ with excellence.
Challenging Christians
to live victoriously,
grow spiritually,
know God intimately.

Connect with us on

f Facebook @ **HarrisonHousePublishers**

and **Instagram** @ **HarrisonHousePublishing**

so you can stay up to date with news

about our books and our authors.

Visit us at **www.harrisonhouse.com**

for a complete product listing as well as

monthly specials for wholesale distribution.